Aliens in Your Native Land

Aliens in Your Native Land
——— 1 Peter and the Formation of Christian Identity ———

Warner M. Bailey

WITH A FOREWORD BY
Stephen V. Sprinkle

☙PICKWICK *Publications* • Eugene, Oregon

ALIENS IN YOUR NATIVE LAND
1 Peter and the Formation of Christian Identity

Copyright © 2020 Warner M. Bailey. All rights reserved. Except for brief quotations in critical publications or reviews, no part of this book may be reproduced in any manner without prior written permission from the publisher. Write: Permissions, Wipf and Stock Publishers, 199 W. 8th Ave., Suite 3, Eugene, OR 97401.

Pickwick Publications
An Imprint of Wipf and Stock Publishers
199 W. 8th Ave., Suite 3
Eugene, OR 97401

www.wipfandstock.com

PAPERBACK ISBN: 978-1-7252-6848-7
HARDCOVER ISBN: 978-1-7252-6849-4
EBOOK ISBN: 978-1-7252-6850-0

Cataloguing-in-Publication data:

Names: Bailey, Warner M., author. | Sprinkle, Stephen V., foreword.

Title: Aliens in your native land : 1 Peter and the formation of Christian identity / by Warner M. Bailey ; foreword by Stephen V. Sprinkle.

Description: Eugene, OR: Pickwick Publications, 2020 | Includes bibliographical references.

Identifiers: ISBN 978-1-7252-6848-7 (paperback) | ISBN 978-1-7252-6849-4 (hardcover) | ISBN 978-1-7252-6850-0 (ebook)

Subjects: LCSH: Bible—Peter, 1st—Criticism, interpretation, etc. | Bible—Minor Prophets—Criticism, interpretation, etc. | Bonhoeffer Dietrich—1906–1945

Classification: BS2795.52 B35 2020 (print) | BS2795.52 (ebook)

All Scriptural texts, except as where noted, are reprinted from the Common Bible: New Revised Standard Version Bible, copyright 1989. Division of Christian Education of the National Council of the Churches of Christ in the United States of America. Used by permission. All rights reserved.

Manufactured in the U.S.A.   07/06/20

This book is dedicated to the congregations of
First Presbyterian Church, Columbus, Indiana
Ridglea Presbyterian Church, Fort Worth, Texas
St. Stephen Presbyterian Church, Fort Worth Texas
Temples of living stones
linked together by the One
in whose trust they will not be put to shame

Contents

Foreword by Stephen V. Sprinkle | ix

Introduction | xiii

Chapter 1: The Authorial Intent of 1 Peter | 1

Chapter 2: The Contribution of the Twelve to the Message of Consolation in 1 Peter | 26

Chapter 3: The Influence of the Twelve on Counter-Intuitive Identity in 1 Peter | 51

Chapter 4: The Use of 1 Peter by Aliens in the Modern Era, Part 1—Dietrich Bonhoeffer | 65

Chapter 5: The Use of 1 Peter by Aliens in the Modern Era, Part 2 | 98

Chapter 6: Conclusions | 116

Bibliography | 131

Foreword

POINTS OF CONTACT BETWEEN actual situations, God-talk, and the practices that address them are the stock and trade of practical theologians. Professionally and personally, I explore life along the blurred boundaries between worlds normally exclusive of each other. Tidal pools and estuaries are a good eco-analogy for the liminal territories practical theologians thrive within. We embrace the binaries of nominally exclusionary existences, interrogate them, and discover the new possibilities that spawn there. Instead of the sea *or* dry land of academic abstraction or practical situations, we want to encounter the richness of the experiences of *both* where formerly incommensurate spheres co-mingle and generate something new and rare. What God is up to along the borderlands and boundary waters of life where differing worlds touch is what a practical theologian seeks to suss out. That is how I came to meet and value the gifts of Warner M. Bailey, the author of this intriguing book.

Warner is not content to confine himself either to the academy or the hurly-burly of congregational life. As an ordained minister of word and sacrament, he has a distinguished record as pastor in Indiana and Texas. I first met him as the senior minister of Fort Worth's Ridglea Presbyterian Church where he carved out a hard-won, citywide reputation as a fine preacher and an advocate for marginalized people. He mentored several students from the supervised ministry program I administer for Brite Divinity School at Texas Christian University as one of our best Field Supervisors. He currently serves as an adjunct faculty member with us, and as director of the Presbyterian Studies program. Warner's desire to write and teach urged him more deeply into scholastic exploration as an essayist and published author. Our bonds of respect and friendship grew because of our mutual rejection of the false dichotomy between scholarship and commitment to the church. I saw in him then, and see in him now, a kindred spirit. His thirst both *to know* and *to do* is too great to prefer one part of the equation above the other. Simply put, he is a scholar-pastor, the genuine article.

Hence, this latest book, *Aliens in Your Native Land: 1 Peter and the Formation of Christian Identity*. Using the first-century CE letter of 1 Peter as the anchor of his concern with human suffering and the formation of Christian identity, Warner carefully builds his case with hermeneutic precision, opening reams of scholarship into the purpose and meaning of the letter to the reader. He leads us to see how the precedents set by the Hebrew testament authors of the Book of the Twelve are drawn upon by 1 Peter to amplify its power to strengthen a faith community under duress. Warner never allows himself to be lost in the weeds of scholarly controversy concerning 1 Peter. He keeps his focus on the main theological question that the original community of faith was struggling to answer on the brink of collapse from harsh imperial pressure: "Will God be faithful in vindicating the Christian's confession of loyalty to Jesus Christ?" Repeatedly, he demonstrates that consolation for those suffering oppression because of their Christian faith is the core purpose of 1 Peter, a theme that unlocks its continuing relevance for the formation of Christian identity today.

But Warner goes a bolder step farther than addressing the perennial anxieties of alienation, unjust oppression, and expulsion from home with which each generation of humanity wrestles. He demonstrates how a robust, new identity takes hold in the lives of believers who face persecution for the sake of their faith, not despite the suffering they endure, but as a result of it. The key dimension that fortifies Christian endurance in oppressive situations is Christological, rooted firmly in the faithfulness of God to Jesus Christ made clear in the passion and the resurrection event—his vindication from God. Warner argues that Christians enduring suffering explicitly for their Christian faith may also trust in their own coming vindication by God. Identification with the Christ revealed in the passion and resurrection goes beyond any sort of therapeutic coping benefits for them. Those who suffer for the sake of Jesus Christ, who bless their oppressors rather than curse them, extend God's offer of reconciliation to the very persecutors of the faithful. Innocently suffering Christians become both an extension of the mercies and merits of the work of Christ, and also an envoy of Christian reconciliation to their tormenter. Thus, the consolation sealed by identification with this deeply mature Christology is *evangelical* in the original sense. It is infused with the Good News of a faith that reconciles a gone-wrong world, and transforms it by means of a creative new hope.

FOREWORD

Though he recognizes that his account of suffering and consolation in 1 Peter is controversial, rather than posturing defensively, Warner engages modern examples of both critics and exemplars of his position. His treatment of Dietrich Bonhoeffer's struggle with Nazi oppression in light of 1 Peter is one of the high points of his book. He also examines feminist, black, and queer interpreters of the letter in order to learn from the marginalized communities they represent, and he deals with their wisdom with fairness, clarity, and humility. One trenchant observation Warner makes about Bonhoeffer's reliance upon faith in the God of resurrection even as he faced despair and execution shows us just how significant 1 Peter's tenacious hope can be for any community of aliens and strangers facing unjust suffering in our own anxiety-ridden age. Noting the "realistic and sober" assessment Bonhoeffer made of the situation marginalized Christians faced in the Third Reich, Warner writes that the practice of returning to 1 Peter in order to encounter God's will "must be preserved for the search for faithfulness in this Trumpian time."

A good practical theologian, faced with the demands of a troublesome situation, moves from what was previously taken for granted through the unknown to a new way of knowing what God is up to in the world . . . , and then the questions raised by this new set of understandings ignites the search to commence once again. Warner Bailey is a skilled searcher for faithfulness like that, one who led me back to read 1 Peter as if for the first time. His book caused me to crack open the first Bible of my youth that I had read with naïve receptiveness, and to pore over note after note I had scribbled on the pages of 1 Peter. And so, then, Warner's skillful guidance moved me to wrestle with the words of that ancient text in dialogue with the scholarly debates and faithful seekers he brings to life on page after page, as a seeker living now in the turmoil of today. That is what masterful biblical interpreters ultimately do. They stretch us, provoke us, and lead us, not to a foregone conclusion of their own making, but like my friend Warner does in this fine book, to read 1 Peter anew—for ourselves.

Stephen V. Sprinkle
Professor of Practical Theology
Brite Divinity School
Fort Worth, Texas

Introduction

THE CHALLENGES OF LIVING as an alien in one's native land are all too well known to marginalized communities. As is becoming clearer every day, these communities of outliers are being joined by people of every stripe who, because of cultural, economic, and political shifts, are finding themselves strangers in their own land, up against a system of greed, hubris, racism, sexism xenophobia, media manipulation, and self-centeredness. The list is interminable.

This book asks the question: what does it mean to live as an alien in your own country? We take up what many feel today as a general sense of homelessness. For example, Arlie Russell Hochschild's book *Strangers in Their Own Land* documents the lived experience of a group of staunchly conservative residents of southwest Louisiana who sense that their "way of life" is being choked off by a circle of threats, ranging from environmental disaster to being looked down upon by liberal elites. Others make the same point: David Brooks writes often of a growing sense of political, cultural, and economic homelessness.[1] Leonard Pitts, Jr. cautions, "Fascism: It CAN Happen Here."[2]

However, this book asks the question with a particular slant: What does it mean to live as an alien in your own country when the cause of your being an alien is your obedience to Jesus Christ as Lord? How can a Christian witness persist under a sustained threat within a social order diametrically opposed to it? This is the question 1 Peter asks which drives the investigation presented here. The implications of its answer are meant to give guidance to faithful ecclesiastical practice and personal witness. We

---

1. See for example, "Will Gen-Z Save the World?" and "A New Center Being Born."
2. *Fort Worth StarTelegram*, October 14, 2019.

will arrive at our answer by investigating the way the author funds the epistles' message from the Book of the Twelve (Hosea-Malachi). The arc of our investigation travels from canonical exegesis through theological reflection to implications for the continued use of 1 Peter to nurture faithfulness. To guide the reader, here is a summary of the way our study proceeds.

In chapter 1 various approaches currently in play to answering the question of why this epistle was written are considered. All have in common a desire to break out beyond the impasse in Petrine studies created by the opposing options set out by the pioneering work of John Elliott and David Balche. We critically examine the contributions of Kelly D. Liebengood, Paul A. Holloway, Steven R. Bechtler, and David G. Horrell. The insights of Holloway and Horrell become the basis for our constructive proposal. From Holloway we affirm his description of 1 Peter as a type of consolation literature common to the Greek-speaking world. Horrell supplies the insightful perspective that the addressees are largely native born rather than forced immigrants who have converted to Christianity.

We contend that 1 Peter is a letter of consolation/comfort written to Christian communities, composed largely of native born believers, in Asia Minor in the turn of the first century CE. These people are experiencing localized persecution because of the political implications of confessing Jesus Christ as Lord. While the author's use of the Old Testament is well documented, what has not been examined carefully is the particular use made of the Book of the Twelve in formulating the content of the comfort the epistle extends to suffering communities. We show that because the Twelve was a long recognized document communicating comfort to the Jewish diaspora, it is very well suited to contribute to the aim of the epistle.

This aim, stated briefly, is to impress on its readers that they will be able to cope with whatever "fiery trials" they may face and remain faithful to their confession because God is undergirding their endurance with God's faithfulness to them. The epistle puts forward Jesus as the one who committed his life to God through the shame and abandonment of the cross, and God vindicated God's faithfulness to him through his resurrection. The epistle claims that the crucified-resurrected Lord embraces within his suffering his persecuted believers in their suffering so that this Lord can share with believers the power that resides in his resurrection. This gives those made subordinate by suffering a new sense of agency, stamina and verve. This behavior even holds promise of converting the oppressors.

INTRODUCTION

Chapter 2 pursues the funding of these claims from the Twelve. We point out hermeneutical strategies which give the author access to the rich deposit of images and narratives in the Twelve. These support crucial aspects of 1 Peter's message of comfort: being born anew (Jonah), sired by the Word (Hosea), a people for his possession (Malachi), not being put to shame (Joel), and fiery trial (Zechariah). Considering the aggregate of these textual linkages begins to suggest a profile of counter-intuitive identity founded on the life and destiny of Jesus Christ.

Chapter 3 widens the influence of the Twelve on the development of the counter-intuitive identity espoused by 1 Peter by examining three texts in Habakkuk, Micah, and Malachi where counter-intuitive identity is being practiced. We suggest the likelihood of the influence of these texts due to the familiarity of the author of 1 Peter over the wide range of the Twelve. Special attention is paid to the experience of worship, shared both by 1 Peter and the Twelve, as the setting for the nurture and shaping of the counter-intuitive identity. Again, the new, counter-intuitive agency which flows from the new identity is part of the presentation of the Twelve as well as 1 Peter. The chapter closes with an examination of the climax of the epistle in 4:13–16 where a densely packed statement of counter-intuitive identity and behavior is located.

Chapter 4 asks the question: Where in the modern world has 1 Peter been accessed by aliens in their native land? We investigate the role 1 Peter played in the life and work of Dietrich Bonhoeffer, giving particular attention to his opposition against Nazism. We discovered nine examples of Bonhoeffer's use of 1 Peter beginning from the persecution of German Jews and concluding with his death. He clearly thought of himself as an alien in his native land. First Peter provides much needed comfort and encouragement to Bonhoeffer. It also supplies the source texts for the theological development of his Christology and soteriology. These are key supports to his exposition of "worldly Christianity" practiced by an alien in his native land. We note that while working almost 100 years before Horrell's breakthrough, nevertheless, Bonhoeffer anticipates his position.

In chapter 5 we continue our exploration of the use communities under threat have made of 1 Peter into the late twentieth and early twenty-first centuries. The models of Elliott, Balch, and Horrell are tested for their ability to guide aliens in their own lands to access 1 Peter in ways that nurture faithfulness. We look at how these models play out within immigrant communities and communities of women, queers, and blacks. In

INTRODUCTION

addition, we introduce a group of international interpreters who write under the stress of being native born aliens. These scholars illustrate the enduring importance of 1 Peter as a tool to describe their present crisis and to offer counsel to their communities for the sake of strengthening their faithfulness. We offer observations as to whether the counsel offered by Elliott, Balch, and Horrell helps threatened communities engage openly with oppressive social and political orders or supports seeing themselves as a sect concerned more for self-protection. The chapter concludes with a critical appraisal of the seminal work of Stanley Hauerwas and William Willimon, *Resident Aliens, Life in the Christian Colony.*

In chapter 6 we bring this investigation to a close by taking up the difficulties 1 Peter presents to certain groups made to feel themselves as native-born aliens through discrimination. We engage feminist, queer, and black critics and their concerns over the counsel 1 Peter gives to slaves and wives and the model of Jesus as a suffering alien. We describe the use these critics make of various strategies of interpretation to circumvent their concerns, and we evaluate how these strategies impinge on the integrity of the letter. We bring forward the notion of an eschatological qualifier as an apt way of 1 Peter's talking about the indestructible power of Jesus as Lord to uphold those who come into his life against the threats leveled at their faithfulness.

Our book concludes with an attempt to identify what it means to be an alien in contemporary America for two large groups of citizens who are keenly aware of their being marginalized: fundamentalist evangelicals and the OK-boomer cohort. Their shared marginalization springs from a common conviction that the trajectory of their lives is on an irreversible decline.

Against interlocking systems of power that are bent on self-aggrandizement to the negligence of those who are left behind and left out, the pressure is immense on the marginalized either to capitulate or to retreat into silence. Increasingly, those who attempt to resist are pushed to the margins where they suffer the consequences for confronting the powerful. 1 Peter is meant in our time for persons and communities who struggle to find the insight to respond to overwhelming odds with energy and new alternatives. "Cast all your anxiety on him, because he cares for you" (5:7).

I express my gratitude to a group of colleagues who have offered valuable advice and counsel in the writing of this book. David J. Gouwens and Thomas W. Currie read earlier drafts of the chapter on Bonhoeffer and made important suggestions in perfecting it. Timothy Sandoval and Ariel Feldman assisted in pointing out possible connections between the Book of the Twelve and communities who read it in the Jewish Diaspora. Timothy Lee introduced me to the use of 1 Peter by Asian immigrant groups in the United States. Charles Bellinger supplied the guidance into the analysis of the collected works of Dietrich Bonhoeffer. Conversations with Gary Dorrien and Will Wilson prompted me to pursue fresh lines of inquiry. I value greatly the conversations with my wife, Mary, about the pastoral implications of the epistle's message.

Finally, I dedicate this book to the congregation of First Presbyterian Church in Columbus, Indiana, and to the congregations of Ridglea Presbyterian Church and St. Stephen Presbyterian Church in Fort Worth, Texas. They have generously supported me over the course of forty-six years of being Minister of Word and Sacrament. Working together, I took on the responsibility and joy of helping to shape these congregations to be temples of living stones linked together by the One in whose trust they will not be put to shame.

1

The Authorial Intent of 1 Peter

WHY WAS 1 PETER COMPOSED and sent to the churches in Anatolia[1] in the waning years of the first century of the common era? Although the question is perennial, in the last fifty years it has been pursued vigorously down diverse trajectories. The path-breaking parallel investigations of John Elliott[2] and David Balch[3] gave interpreters a choice between two strikingly different alternatives.[4]

Broadly speaking, Elliott's answer claims that the letter is directed to Christians forcibly removed from their homelands and relocated in diaspora. The letter's purpose is to foster internal cohesion among the community of believers in order to build as exiles a distinctive communal identity and resist external pressures to conform. The readers of the letter are to think of themselves as a sect of converts that resists, as much as possible, contact with the social world in which they live. The world is an evil and hostile place to this sect, but nonetheless, the sect considers itself to have a missionary task to save individuals from this wicked world through conversion.

In Balch's view, the letter counsels Christians to engage positively, as much as possible, with non-Christian neighbors. "The purpose of 1 Peter, and specifically its domestic code, was to lessen the hostility and antagonism

---

1. For introductory questions of authorship and setting, see the standard commentaries.

2. Beginning in 1966 with *The Elect and the Holy*, culminating in 2000 with his commentary in the Anchor Bible series.

3. *Let Wives Be Submissive*.

4. David Horrell presents a balanced assessment of this impasse. The following four paragraphs are drawn from his "Between Conformity and Resistance," 112–17. See also Feldmeier, *The First Letter of Peter*, 13, "The alienation from the world is not from the negating of the world but as the flip side of belonging to God."

suffered by Christians by urging them to demonstrate their conformity to conventional social expectations. The church, in other words, was to accommodate to the world, in order to reduce the tensions between them."[5]

Both options assume in common that the addressees largely come from populations that are not native to Anatolia. They are in Asia Minor as a result of imperial, forced migration. However, recently this assumption has been under increasing challenge. David Horrell, among others, has pointed out "converts seem to be mostly Gentiles and have previously been well accustomed to the way of life of their wider society, a way of life from which they *now* are urged to distance themselves. These are not, then, people for whom the wider culture is alien and strange, but people whose conversion to Christianity has *created* an alienation, the consequences of which need to be worked out."[6] Faced with this challenge, scholarly attention has been drawn to whether the models of assimilation/acculturation (Balch) or sectarian withdrawal (Elliott) are appropriate to describe the letter's idea of how Christians should negotiate their place in society.

A major breakthrough of this impasse was mounted by Horrell who noticed that "what is most obviously missing from both these social-scientific approaches—and from most other attempts to move beyond the Balch-Elliott debate—is explicit attention to the structures of (imperial) domination with which the addresses of 1 Peter must negotiate their conformity and/or their resistance to the world." Horrell grasped that at the heart of the letter is the believer's coming to grips with the criminalization of confessing Christ.[7] He pinpointed that in order to develop and sustain Christian character in the context of criminalization a re-valuing of this name into an honorable badge of new identity was required.

Horrell and others took note of how the sustained use of the Old Testament in 1 Peter contributes to the strategy of revaluation necessary to maintaining stamina and verve in the face of potential persecution. Because Jesus Christ so identified with Israel's story, those who follow him can draw from Israel's story of the faithfulness of God. Israel's story, therefore,

---

5 Warren Carter would go much farther in this direction, holding that the letter supports a broad accommodation to prevailing social practice as a survival strategy. See "'Going all the Way?'"

6. Horrell, "Between Conformity and Resistance," 116.

7. Horrell "The Label Χριστιανός," 361–81. For a description of the antipathy toward Christians see Holloway, *Coping with Prejudice*, 55, 65. He points out that κακοποιῶν which is typically translated "evildoer" had ancient connotations something more like "criminal." 67.

becomes a major factor supporting Christian identity under threat.⁸ This study focuses on how that portion of Israel's scripture, Hosea through Malachi, which taken together in a canonical way are called The Book of the Twelve,⁹ is used by 1 Peter in the strategy of revaluation.

Horrell's work has created subsequent investigations into the authorial intent, or the driving question, of 1 Peter. A discussion and evaluation of three examples of divergent answers which have been offered in the last ten years will provide the context for our constructive proposal.

1 Peter as an Explanation of Suffering

Kelly Liebengood mounts the case that "the precise issue with which Peter and his addresses are struggling [is] if Jesus is in the fact the Christ, the agent appointed to bring about restoration, then why are we suffering *after* his coming?"¹⁰ The characterization in 1 Peter of this suffering as a period of "fiery trials" (4:12) alerts Liebengood to the allusion being made to Zech 13:9 ("And I will put this third into the fire and refine them as on refines silver and test them as gold is tested"). The resonating of Zech 13:9 in 1 Peter suggests to Liebengood that the author of 1 Peter may have drawn more extensively from the eschatological program of Zech 9–14 to help Christians know why they are still suffering after Jesus' resurrection. In his discussion of the Zechariahan material, Liebengood demonstrates a significant impulse to the shaping of 1 Peter.

The basic contours of the distinctive eschatological program of Zechariah 9–14 are: "YHWH's shepherd will suffer a death that will serve to cleanse 'the house of God' upon which the Spirit now rests; (4:14) and bring back the scattered sheep to God, while also placing them in a period of fiery trials that they must endure until final consummation."¹¹ Through a sensitive and far-reaching program of exegesis, Liebengood describes how major points of Zechariah's eschatological program form the substructure of 1 Peter, even though there is no explicit mention of Zechariah in 1 Peter. Against this inconsistency, he argues "that reflective discourse, such as the kind we find in 1 Peter, can at times be governed by

---

8. Horrell "Whose Faithfulness," 110–15.
9. See Bailey, *Living in the Language of God*.
10. Liebengood, *The Eschatology of 1 Peter*, 206.
11. Liebengood, *The Eschatology of 1 Peter*, 177–78.

a foundational narrative that may find only allusive fragmentary expression within the discourse itself."[12]

First Peter's Christology, for example, draws upon significant Zechariahan texts 10:2 (LXX); 11:4–17; 12:10; and 13:7 to present the work of Jesus as causational.

> Jesus Christ has caused something to happen—as a result of his sacrificial death, the addressees have been relationally restored to God and presently are awaiting an inheritance, which will be awarded at the return of Jesus Christ. In the meantime, as the renewed people of God, they now find themselves living in a transition period characterized both as fiery trials in which their fidelity to God will be rested as well as a wilderness/second exodus journey towards their prepared inheritance.[13]

Liebengood's position is that 1 Peter counsels that suffering can be endured when the Christian recognizes that it is a part of the plan of God's will, written in the scriptures of the prophets: "Concerning this salvation, the prophets who prophesied of the grace that was to be yours made careful search and inquiry" (1:10) and "For it stands in scripture" (2:6).[14] Anatolian Christians are called to trust in the outworking of the plan as the foundation for negotiating "their allegiance to Jesus in a social context that, for a number of reasons, is antagonistic to such a commitment."[15]

Liebengood offers a fresh reading of 1 Peter that addresses explicitly the context of oppression being experienced by its readers. He illustrates how prophetic material is made to speak again to create a framework for remaining faithful to Christ. He senses rightly the strong eschatological grounding of the epistle's counsel. The probity of his position, however, depends upon the cohesion of several unique exegetical decisions, anyone of which is subject to dispute.

My concern is not to evaluate exegetical decisions, but to concentrate at the foundational level. In the course of this book I will contend that the question at the heart of the letter is framed differently than Liebengood's construction. Before engaging with Liebengood I will state what I propose to defend. *Given the experience of suffering because one is charged with the*

---

12. Liebengood, *The Eschatology of 1 Peter*, 215.
13. Liebengood, *The Eschatology of 1 Peter*, 218.
14. Liebengood, *The Eschatology of 1 Peter*, 206.
15. Liebengood, *The Eschatology of 1 Peter*, 175. See also 190, 198.

offense of being a Christian,[16] *the most urgent question is: will God be faithful in vindicating the Christian's confession of loyalty to Jesus Christ?* Can Christians trust God to uphold them in their trial by torture and the threat of certain death? In the pages that follow, I will show that 1 Peter consistently demonstrates the relationship of divine faithfulness undergirding human faithfulness. This, to me, provides the most satisfactory answer to the question: can God's faithfulness be counted on in vindicating Christians who confess loyalty to Jesus under pain of suffering? Such is the burden of why "I have written this short letter to encourage you" (1 Pet 5:12). It is from this position that Liebengood will be engaged.

Liebengood affirms that 1 Peter aims at forming moral character and active dependence on God, by appealing to a plan revealed in scripture. By relying on a plan, readers might endure in the midst of suffering.[17] Whereas the notion of a plan does supply the important ingredient of an end-point, and a plan functions as an antidote to the panic of chaos, this is not the dominant concern in 1 Peter. We cannot detect in 1 Peter a clearly laid out plan drawn from Zech 9–14 to accomplish this aim of shoring up moral character. Even though early Christians did search the Old Testament to discern answers to questions of unexplained suffering, we are not convinced that Anatolian Christians were asking the question as it is framed by Liebengood: "if Jesus is in fact the Christ, the agent appointed to bring about restoration, then why are we suffering after his coming?"[18]

An overreliance on the strength of a plan has shaped significantly three of Liebengood's principle conclusions.

First, reliance on a plan derived from scripture as the final explanation to the believer's question of why, after Jesus has risen, we must suffer, affects the reader's orientation to the authority of scripture. In perhaps his strongest statement, Liebengood asserts, "And finally, and perhaps most importantly, we are able to discern that Peter's principal strategy for helping his addressees thrive in the midst of suffering and social alienation is to show them that what they are undergoing is κατὰ τὰς γραφὰς (according to what is written), and in particular κατὰ Ζαχαρίαν 9–14."[19] That is to say, the printed record, trust in the printed record, is to be seen by addressees

---

16. Horrell, "Between Conformity and Resistance," 138–39.
17. See Dryden, *Theology and Ethics in 1 Peter*, 37–55.
18. Liebengood, *The Eschatology of 1 Peter*, 206.
19. Liebengood, *The Eschatology of 1 Peter*, 214.

as proof enough for them to persevere. Consequently, trust in a living relationship between God and God's people is diminished.

Second, this reliance on proof from the printed word impacts Liebengood's presentation of the person and work of Jesus. Jesus comes across as the primary trigger to the unfolding of that plan. Seeing Jesus as the plan's First Cause can shift the attention of the reader from what is repeatedly emphasized in 1 Peter, which is: the example of the trust Jesus reposed in the faithfulness of God. This is what the believer clings to as reason for maintaining their allegiance to Jesus under pressure.

Third, under the influence of a plan, the letter's counsel could be summed up as encouragement to hold on until the final restoration. Such counsel tends to shift the burden of performance onto the individual believer. On the contrary, the epistle demonstrates the good news of the performance of God's commitment to Jesus, demonstrated in the eschatological event of the resurrection. It advances this fact as the grounds for the believer's banking on the commitment of God to be faithful in supporting believers under severe testing. The believer's relationship with Jesus is the substance of the "living hope" that grounds and protects the believer's holding on.

The question that grounds the pastoral counsel of 1 Peter is not "why are we suffering after Christ has risen?" as Liebengood suggests, but a more existential question "can we trust in a faithful God when we must suffer for the (criminal) charge of being a Christian?" This changes our appreciation of how 1 Peter uses the imagery of the fiery trial from Zechariah. If that prophecy is not appealed to for an explanation of a stage in God's plan, we owe an explanation of how the letter's allusion to a period of fiery trials supports his pastoral counsel of demonstrating the faithfulness of God as an encouragement for believers under severe testing. We will address this later as we consider the full impact of the use the writer of 1 Peter makes of the collection Hosea-Malachi as it has been canonically shaped to be the Book of the Twelve.

In sum, the letter's counsel is directed to deepening the undergirding faithfulness that grows out of the believer's relationship with Jesus. Therefore, before proceeding to the next alternative, it is important to fill out this foundational theme of God's undergirding faithfulness in 1 Peter.

1 Peter as a Demonstration of Divine Faithfulness Undergirding Human Faithfulness

Certainly this is uppermost at the opening of the letter. First Peter 1:2 calls the exiles of the Dispersion "chosen and destined by God the Father," language that bears the imprint of settled divine decision. In the following verses this notion is developed to bind God's decision with the believer's trust in God. The chosen and destined exiles are guarded by God's power through God's faithfulness for salvation (1:5).[20] They may rejoice that they are able to rest confidently in God's faithfulness when occasions arise to test their faith, knowing that the genuineness of their faith redounds to the praise, honor and glory of God (1:7–8). Furthermore, the resurrection of Jesus from the dead, the *sine qua non* of God's faithfulness to him, produces in the believers a living hope which is kept alive by focusing on an inheritance which is imperishable, undefiled and unfading—qualities only associated with divine faithfulness (1:3–4).[21] The writer concludes this introductory section of the letter by an *inclusio* in 1:21 underlining the centrality of Jesus as the one through whom believers come to trust in God. His resurrection from the dead proves God's ability to be faithful. Clearly the coordination of human and divine faithfulness is a driving force in the letter's opening pastoral outreach to support exiles and aliens who are suffering.

Again, in 2:4–8, which is crucial for establishing the new identity of the "aliens and exiles," Isa 28:16 is quoted and interpreted as alluding to Jesus as "a cornerstone, chosen and precious" providing the foundation upon which the living stones of believers are built into a spiritual house. The aspect of divine solidarity which the cornerstone communicates is specifically focused on encouraging the believers by the concluding words of Isa 28:16, "and he who believes in him will not be put to shame." This major emphasis in the epistle is examined more closely.

1. Honor and Shame in 1 Peter

The introduction of the notion of shame serves to anchor the solidarity with Jesus within the very real experience of the honor-shame codes that permeated the social world of early Christians and their neighbors. Pliny's letter

---

20. Horrell "Whose Faithfulness," 110–15.

21. See the creedal expression in 3:18 "put to death indeed in the flesh but nevertheless made alive in the Spirit."

to the emperor Trajan, which is often cited as providing the clearest description of the facts-on-the-ground background to 1 Peter, makes explicit mention of how informers on Christians publicly expose and shame them through anonymous methods, a practice which Trajan decidedly rejects as inadmissible in a prosecution of criminal charges against Christians.[22] Here are the relevant paragraphs of the letter:

> Meanwhile, in the case of those who were denounced to me as Christians, I have observed the following procedure: I interrogated these as to whether they were Christians; those who confessed I interrogated a second and a third time, threatening them with punishment; those who persisted I ordered executed. For I had no doubt that, whatever the nature of their creed, stubbornness and inflexible obstinacy surely deserve to be punished. There were others possessed of the same folly; but because they were Roman citizens, I signed an order for them to be transferred to Rome.
>
> Soon accusations spread, as usually happens, because of the proceedings going on, and several incidents occurred. An anonymous document was published containing the names of many persons. Those who denied that they were or had been Christians, when they invoked the gods in words dictated by me, offered prayer with incense and wine to your image, which I had ordered to be brought for this purpose together with statues of the gods, and moreover cursed Christ—none of which those who are really Christians, it is said, can be forced to do—these I thought should be discharged. Others named by the informer declared that they were Christians, but then denied it, asserting that they had been but had ceased to be, some three years before, others many years, some as much as twenty-five years. They all worshipped your image and the statues of the gods, and cursed Christ.

Honor-shame codes become a crucial ingredient in Seven Bechtler's explanation of why 1 Peter was written, the second of the three proposals we are examining. "In the light of the honor-shame model . . . the nature of the suffering engendered by . . . hostile speech came into sharper relief. The slanderous accusation and verbal challenges directed at 1 Peter's addresses actually constituted a threat to their honor and social status. The

---

22. Pliny the Younger was governor of Pontus/Bithynia from 111 to 113 AD. He corresponded frequently with the emperor Trajan on a variety of administrative political matters. In this correspondence Pliny encounters Christianity for the first time. Pliny, *Letters* 10. 96–97. See, Holloway, *Coping with Prejudice*, 47 for a summary of Pliny's letter and discussion of its importance.

suffering with which 1 Peter deals, therefore, is the relentless attack on honor in the form of slander in general and false accusations of wrongdoing in particular."[23] They have been shamed and have lost honor as a result of their break from their former "world." Now because their fiery trial has made them lose honor, their stamina to live in their new "world"—as aliens in their native land—is very much in doubt. Bechtler contends that the shamed believers can persist because as God bestowed honor on the suffering Jesus in the resurrection, God has promised new honor at the return of Jesus to the shamed Christian. Even now, this new honor, by the Spirit, can be anticipated. However, it will only be fully bestowed at the return of Jesus as the result of unswerving belief in Jesus throughout one's life.[24] Jesus is the model Christian to be followed. This, Bechtler argues, is 1 Peter's counsel to those suffering the "fiery trial."

Bechtler sees 1 Pet 2:4–10 providing "the fundamental nexus of relations and oppositions among Christ, his followers, and their detractors that will provide the means by which challenges to honor coming from non-Christians can be evaluated and countered within the Christian communities."[25] He identifies 2:6 "put to shame" with the outsiders' attacks on the addresses' honor. The epistle states in both negative and positive ways, that those who believe in Jesus will counter this challenge: negatively, that they will "not be put to shame," and positively that "Honor is granted to them."[26] Bechtler draws out the implications for this positive reading of ὑμῖν οὖν ἡ τιμὴ τοῖς πιστεύουσιν: "In the immediate context it is not so much a question of how Christian believers perceive Christ as of how God . . . perceives him, and of how God consequently vindicates both Christ and his followers."[27]

Betchler has identified a central and compelling concern of the addressees. However, my reading of the epistle reaches the opposite conclusion. I translate ὑμῖν οὖν ἡ τιμὴ τοῖς πιστεύουσιν as "To you who believe, [he, (Christ)] is [your] honor." Certainly, it is more straightforward to pair the preciousness of the cornerstone in 2:6 with the preciousness/honor of Christ in 2:7. Bechtler sees honor and shame as two distinct symbol-worlds, and God can give to shamed believers the honor bestowed on Christ in his

23. Bechtler, *Following in His Steps*, 106.
24. Bechtler, *Following in His Steps*, 185–87.
25. Bechtler, *Following in His Steps*, 186.
26. Bechtler, *Following in His Steps*, 187.
27. Bechtler, *Following in His Steps*, 187. Quoting from Michaels, *1 Peter*, 104.

resurrection to displace partially the shame of their fiery trial. This becomes the incentive to hold out for a full inheritance of honor at Christ's return.

However, the text does not make a simple contrast between honor to the believers and dishonor to the unbelievers. What is contrasted is the way that Christ is simultaneously honor to the believer and dishonor to the unbeliever. As Boring points out, "Being rejected and crucified was not an episode in the career of Jesus, that was put behind him by the Resurrection. He continues through history as the Rejected One, modeling the present status of his disciples." [28] Therefore, we must seek a different way of relating honor and shame, a Christology that reflects the simultaneous presence of both honor and shame in Christ.

First Peter emphasizes that an exposed person will not be put to shame through belief in Jesus. This assertion only makes sense if the shame which is avoided is different in kind from that which will be experienced in the shamed one's social world. I have shown elsewhere that the context of shaming referenced in this text is theological.[29] The horrific experience of being publicly ambushed, exposed, shamed, and prosecuted always contains the live threat of tipping over into the devastating conclusion that God has shamed the targeted one through abandonment. The experience of being abandoned transforms the shame of exposure into an existential collapse. [30]

What is at stake here, then, is not the honor of Christians on the sociological level. What is on trial is the honor of God in being able to sustain in Christians an unshakable sense of God's faithfulness in the midst of their collapse of sociological honor. God's test of honor is worked out within the being of God and displayed in the example of Jesus who entrusted himself to God through God's shame and dishonor on the cross and was vindicated in God's resurrecting him from the grave. Those who believe in Jesus Christ, who cast themselves on him utterly, will see their shame and

---

28. Boring, *1 Peter*. 97.

29. For being put to shame as being abandoned, see Bailey, *The Self-Shaming God*.

30. 2 Timothy, written contemporaneously to 1 Peter, is a letter by a mentor who is the target of state prosecution to a protégé encouraging him to resist being swept away in the surge of erstwhile friends abandoning the criminal. In the context of honor-shame influences, the mentor states that he is not ashamed and his protégé should not be either. The reason lies squarely in the personal relation the mentor has with Jesus whose resurrection brings to light the hope of living beyond shame: "For I know in whom I have believed, and I am sure that he is able to guard until that Day what has been entrusted to me" (1:12) See Bailey, *The Self-Shaming God*, 76–77.

dishonor mirrored in his and find in that bond, new stamina, new agency, new hope. First Peter asks its readers to look to Jesus' example and promises those who cleave to him that even though they endure shaming publicly, they will not be shamed through being abandoned by God. "To you then who believe, [he] is [your] honor" (2:7).

As the connection is solidified between the faithfulness of God and the believer's remaining faithful, so the author of 1 Peter makes the connection between the honor of Christ given to believers (2:7) and their acting upon Christ's honor (2:12): "Conduct yourselves honorably among the Gentiles, so that, though they malign you as evildoers, they may see your honorable deeds and glorify God on the day of visitation." Though Christians are stripped of honor in public maligning, they are filled with the honor of Christ and may act out of that resource. We proceed now to look more closely at this central anchor of Christology.

2. The Christological Nexus between Faithfulness and Loyalty

The Christological meeting point between God's faithfulness to the believer and Christians being loyal to Jesus receives its clearest expression in the following section of 1 Pet 2:21-23, which describes the behavior of those who, because they bear the name Christian, have become aliens and exiles to their social world. The base line is: Christ suffered for us, leaving us an example, that we should follow in his steps. "When he suffered, he did not threaten; but he entrusted himself to him who judges justly." It is the example of Jesus' trusting in God through the experience of suffering that provides the clearest evidence of the believer's relationship to Jesus as the foundation of stamina under testing. Believers are to bind themselves to this Jesus as the only way to persevere, as is expressed in the counsel of 3:14-15, "Do not fear what they fear; and do not be intimidated, but in your hearts sanctify Christ as Lord."

First Peter focuses on this relationship as the interpretative framework to manage what his readers are experiencing, and not on the framework of a plan derived from Zechariah. His readers may or may not encounter suffering, but if they do, it is because of their relationship to Jesus and his sufferings, not because that suffering is a necessary phase or stage in the outworking of a divine plan.

At the same time, 1 Pet 2:21–23 signals a new departure setting out how the example of Jesus's trust in God relates to life within the community of aliens and strangers. This new departure had already been in preparation as early as chapter 1, as can be seen through comparing 1:3 and 1:22–23. First Peter 1:3 orients the reader on the person-centered focus of divine election, "we have been born anew into a living hope through the resurrection of Jesus from the dead." In a coordinated fashion, 1 Pet 1:16 brings out the personal ethical lineaments of this election by citing the quotation from Lev 19:2 "Be holy as I am holy."

First Peter 1:22–23 launches a new perspective. Now the personal aspect of divine-human reciprocity moves to community life, "we have been born anew—not from perishable sperm, but from imperishable [a metaphor for the living and remaining word of God]—so that you have genuine mutual love [and can] love one another deeply from the heart."[31]

This early mention of the implications for a communal living out of the divine-human correspondence resurfaces in 2:21–23 in two difficult cases of believing slaves and unbelieving masters and wives who are believers and husbands who are not. In each case, masters and husbands had unquestioned power to choose the gods their household would worship. Therefore, Christians who were not in dominant roles, such as wives and slaves, were in precarious situations of defying not only their superior but also of putting the entire household in a negative light vis-à-vis a society oriented around the male's role in leading his household in religious practices supporting imperial aims.[32] In each case, the believer is directed to the pioneering example of Jesus. He, in similar circumstances, entrusted his life to the one who reserves final judgment, an act which receives further elaboration later in 3:12 ("For the eyes of the Lord are on the righteous, and his ears are open to their prayer. But the face of the Lord is against those who do evil").

---

31. The injunctions to ethical behavior in 2:1–3 and 3:8–12 have their theological footing in this new birth into the living hope through annealing oneself to the faithfulness of God seen in the resurrected Jesus.

32 Feldmeier, "1 Peter and the 'Nation' of Strangers," 253–54. "For the ancients, religion was a public affair, the spiritual basis of state and society. Each person could believe what he wished, the essential thing being that due regard was shown for the received religion and thereby also to the *mos maiorum* Christians were a group that disputed the sacral foundations of state and society which were determinative for the whole of antiquity. The new belief and the new community formed by it invaded the hitherto prevailing social relationships and threatened to destroy them."

This act of giving over one's self creates a new agency in the one who has so yielded herself. The believer's entrustment to Jesus gives access, in an astonishing way, to a freedom not to be defined by the dominant one's enmity, with the consequent possibility of an asymmetrical engagement of non-retaliation, as 1 Pet 2:22 and 3:9 make plain: "When he [Jesus] was abused, he did not return abuse; when he suffered, he did not threaten; but he entrusted himself to the one who judges justly . . . . Do not repay evil for evil or abuse for abuse; but, on the contrary, repay with a blessing. It is to this you were called—that you might inherit a blessing." Miroslav Volf observes: "[1 Pet 3:9] speaks of sovereign serenity and sets a profound revaluation in motion. When blessing replaces rage and revenge, the one who suffers violence refuses to retaliate in kind and chooses instead to encounter violence with an embrace . . . . Only those who refuse to be defined by their enemies can bless them." The consequence of this freedom is that the believer opens up the possibility of even the opponent coming to perceive a different way of life which runs counter to what is conventionally expected.[33]

3. Counter-Intuitive Identity

In the concluding section of 4:12–19 we find a concentration of expressions of how the believer's relationship with Jesus plays a crucial role as the basis for answering the question: Will God be faithful to us when we are subjected to suffering for the offense of being called Christian?[34] This relationship is described in three assertions which reframe a frightening future in counter-intuitive terms. (1) Rejoice in the face of the fiery ordeal because the fellowship of Christ's sufferings is the assurance of rejoicing at the revelation of his glory, vv. 12–13. (2) You are blessed when you are reviled for the name of Christ because the Spirit of glory and of God rests on you, v. 14. (3) Do not be ashamed, but call it an honor, when charged with the offense of being a Christian, because this name honors God, v. 16. These three assertions are rooted in the oscillating dynamic in which those who suffer for the sake of a faithful creator entrust themselves to a faithful creator, v. 19. We will more carefully examine this important reorientation in chapter 3.

It should be evident that the eschatological thrust to these three counter-intuitive statements in 4:12–19 is designed to convey the assurance that

33. Volf, "Soft Difference," 21–22.
34. Horrell "The Label Χριστιανός," 361–81.

counter-intuitive identity already holds within it eschatological blessings. These blessings are currently experienced counter-intuitively as perseverance under fire, but will be revealed openly in all their richness at Christ's coming.[35] Consequently, in the engagement with testing, the believer even now has access to an array of behaviors (joy, blessing, honor) which thwart the intention of those who would use fear and pain to make the believer collapse. It is therefore not the case that one must successfully endure the fiery trial to get access to these blessings. The believer is placed now within this eschatological field of force by virtue of being born anew.[36]

Early on at 1:8–9 this counter-intuitive way of living is sketched vividly. "Although you have not seen him, you love him; and even though you do not see him now, you believe in him and rejoice with an indescribable and glorious joy, for you are receiving the outcome of your faith, the salvation of your souls." This text is crucial for the counter-factual thrust of the epistle. Feldmeier comments, "In this believing trust in the concealed Christ, the contrast between presence and absence is surpassed by the personal relationship to him. That is immediately taken up into the self-understanding of the believers,[37] because their faith and their love are now interpreted as fellowship with the Christ who is withdrawn from their eyes. In faith and love, the (yet) absent one is (already) present to them—and therefore their present is filled with [eschatological] joy."[38]

This mutual interplay between the human act of entrustment and the undergirding of divine faithfulness is so important that it is repeated in the concluding sentences of the letter "Cast all your anxiety on him, because he cares for you" (5:7). Finally, the author brings the letter to a close with a fresh restatement of its opening claims. As the letter opened praising the living hope produced in the believers by the resurrection of Jesus from the dead, a hope defined as an imperishable, undefiled and unfading inheritance, (1:3–4) so it closes in 5:9–11 by a final directive to the readers to be "steadfast in

---

35. On the reframing of how to interpret fiery trials see Horrell "The Label Χριστιανός," Liebengood, *The Eschatology of 1 Peter*, 181 and Feldmeier, *First Letter of Peter*, 95.

36. For additional comment see the discussion of "eschatological qualifiers" in chapter 6.

37. Feldmeier, *First Letter of Peter*, 89–90, investigates the meaning of "soul" in the context of Hellenistic Judaism and suggests that it stands for "the innermost center and 'higher self' of the human being, perhaps similar to the 'hidden person of the heart' (3:4)."

38. Feldmeier, *First Letter of Peter*, 86.

your faith," coupled with a solemn statement of a divine guarantee which outlasts a time of suffering. God's guarantee promises that sufferers will be restored, supported, strengthened, and established. The theme of mutuality is carried forward to the end with the pairing of the call to the believer to be "steadfast" (στερεοί) with the guarantee that the believer will be "supported" (στηρίζει), "To him be the power forever and ever. Amen."

Certainly, the dynamics of the interplay between divine and human faithfulness runs throughout the letter and provides its unifying theme. The appearance of this theme constantly in the context of trial and testing serves as an answer to the fundamental questions which drive the production of the letter: *Given the experience of suffering because one is charged with the offense of being a Christian, will God be faithful in vindicating the Christian's confession of loyalty to Jesus Christ? Can God be trusted to uphold Christians in their being tried by torture and even death? Does the Christian have to worry about being "put to shame" by God's abandonment in the hour of greatest need?*

First Peter was written to give good counsel and comfort. To those experiencing shame, the letter puts forward the figure of Jesus and the call of the gospel to ground one's life in his as the way to neutralize the devastating effects of shame. This, in turn, gives the believer access to a new identity and agency that is anchored in the eschatological power of the resurrection. The purpose of 1 Peter, therefore, allows us to situate the letter within a broader context of contemporaneous writing for consolation.

1 Peter as Consolation Literature

In the first century the kinds of questions generated by suffering were typically addressed through a genre called consolation literature. As early as 1931, Stein demonstrated that in the first century CE, rabbinic homilies regularly ended with words of comfort.[39] The function of the contents of the peroration, as exemplified by several of Philo's tractates, was to offer encouragement of an eschatological nature, such as the Messiah's advent or the restoration of Israel or the world to come.[40]

Following Stein's lead, William Schutter began an investigation of 1 Peter as the product of rabbinic midrash homiletic put to the service of writing an emergency pastoral letter to a circle of churches experiencing a

---

39. Cited in Schutter, *Hermeneutics and Composition*, 99.
40. Schutter, *Hermeneutic and Composition*, 170.

crisis of localized persecution. The author's pressing concern is to speak a word of comfort and advice in his pastoral capacity.[41] The author's exegesis of the prophets yields the theme of the contrast between sufferings and consummation exemplified chiefly in Jesus. This theme becomes for the author a kind of schema which helps to organize Old Testament references throughout the letter. Thus the interplay between suffering and future glory informs Schutter's description of 1:13—2:10 as an exhortation to readers under fiery trials, after the manner of Jewish homiletic midrash, to be holy as the Lord is holy.[42]

Whereas Liebengood frames his investigation by asking how 1 Peter responds to urgent questions circulating within the congregation, in contrast, Schutter does not identify an overriding pastoral question that gives focus and clarity to understanding the epistle. He sees its purpose more broadly, to clarify and buttress Christian conduct with exhortations bolstered by promises of eschatological glory for being faithful and destruction of one's enemies.[43]

Schutter's contribution was to display how a homiletic midrash hermeneutic might have created the content of 1 Peter, though a question remains as to the extent a largely Gentile audience would understand this thoroughly Jewish handling of scripture. However, other questions can be directed to his work as well: Does a concentration on the mechanics of interpretation finally obscure the pastoral issues to which the epistle brings comfort? Examples are: the day to day struggle to incorporate the radical nature of clinging to an absent savior, or the nature of the threat to trust in the integrity of God. Does the concentration on the schema of suffering/glory obscure the deep web which interpersonal divine faithfulness weaves with human faithfulness? Even with these reservations, Schutter must be recognized as one of the first recent interpreters to bring attention to the literary character of 1 Peter as consolation literature.

In contrast to the encouraging thrust of Judaic consolation pieces, the primary object of Greco-Roman consolation literature was to offer help in

---

41 Schutter, *Hermeneutic and Composition*, 176.

42 Schutter, *Hermeneutic and Composition*, 170. He finds 1:10—2:9 "to be infused with a distinctively apocalyptic coloring. Its eschatological outlook, conception of time-periodization, concern for the disclosure of heavenly knowledge through special intermediaries, elaborate pneumatology, and emphasis on Messianic salvation, for example, virtually necessitate an origin for its hermeneutic in sectarian Judaism with a decidedly apocalyptic orientation."

43 Schutter, *Hermeneutic and Composition*, 170-77

overcoming grief and loss, with a secondary goal of regulating the public expression of the emotion of grief. Paul Holloway has advanced the study of 1 Peter by describing the epistle as a type of consolation literature that offers help in coping with the grief of being the object of prejudice based on a stigma.[44] For Holloway, the question driving 1 Peter is: How does one cope with the social prejudice of being identified as a Christian?[45] We will now examine this third approach to understanding 1 Peter.

Holloway identifies two concentrations of consoling material at the beginning and end of 1 Peter. We will only mention the most prominent evidence.

At the beginning of the epistle, the readers' suffering is frankly acknowledged and is redirected in 1:6–7 to become evidence which shows the sufferer's genuineness of faith that redounds to God's praise, honor and glory. This final result has a corollary in an inheritance, undefiled and imperishable kept in heaven for those under trial. Therefore, consolation comes in the instruction to rejoice in the midst of pain.[46]

However, for Holloway the theme of being born to an apocalyptic family plays the major role in providing consolation. This amounts to a reframing of one's narrative wherein a person holds to an apocalyptic world view which understands this present age as evil and sets one's hopes on the revelation of the grace of Christ in the apocalyptic denouement. Such a hope compensates for the shame of the stigma of being criminalized as a Christian. "The new birth attaches the readers to that apocalyptic future which renders them 'sojourners' in this world."[47]

Toward the end of the epistle, the phrase "do not be surprised at the fiery ordeal that is taking place" (4:12) is a clear indication that the letter falls into the genre of consolation literature. Holloway connects this advice to the Cyrenaic maxim *nihil inopinati accidisse* ("nothing unexpected has happened") which figures heavily in the consolation practices of Cicero (106–43 BCE). This maxim is to be followed with the aim of lessening the shock when grief or misfortune happens. By "contemplating the onset of future evils" one eliminates the element of surprise and dilutes the intensification of anguish when disaster occurs. For those already afflicted with grief, consolation lay in the knowledge that "nothing unexpected has

---

44. Holloway, *Coping with Prejudice*.
45. Holloway, *Coping with Prejudice*, 40 and passim.
46. Holloway, *Coping with Prejudice*, 148.
47. Holloway, *Coping with Prejudice*, 131, 138, 139, and chapters 6 and 7.

happened."⁴⁸ The maxim was applied widely in Greek and Jewish philosophy and appears in Paul and John.⁴⁹ Other consolatory words occur in 4:16 "do not consider [suffering] a disgrace" and 4:19 "let those suffering . . . entrust themselves to a faithful God."

By studying 1 Peter as a type of consolation literature, Holloway has opened a new front in grasping the intent and message of the letter. As we have already noted, investigators commonly appeal to the letter of the governor Pliny to the emperor Trajan to gain an appreciation of the peril in which early followers of Jesus found themselves with the consequent pressure to recant. Holloway uses Horrell's demonstration of the criminalizing force of the label "Christian" to expose its prejudicial, stigmatizing consequences.[50] In 1 Pet 4:15–16 suffering as a Christian is placed on par with suffering as a murderer.[51] One of the aims of consolation literature is to support the task of maintaining one's integrity when faced with such labeling.

Holloway's conclusion is that 1 Peter helps its readers cope with the prejudice directed against them for confessing Christ by offering an alternative narrative which allows them to reframe their perilous existence in self-affirming ways. Through the new status of being a sojourner, the stigmatized person gains access to powerful coping resources. Holloway borrows from modern studies of coping with prejudice to bring forward the term "psychological disidentification." He explains: "Disidentification thus entails two operations: (1) rejecting a particular value domain and (2) replacing that domain with a substitute. The sojourner (1) resides in a land that is not one's own while (2) possessing a separate [apocalyptic] homeland where one's true loyalties and aspirations lie."[52]

Holloway has made a major contribution by moving the discussion of the intent of 1 Peter beyond the impasse of understanding it either as a letter written to encourage a sectarian religion or as an encouragement to non-natives to accommodate to the dominant culture.[53] Legitimate questions can be raised, to be sure, about the wisdom of applying modern psychological theories on coping with prejudice to ancient situations. Despite

---

48. Holloway, *Coping with Prejudice*, 85. See also 215–16.

49. Holloway, *Coping with Prejudice*, 218–19.

50. Horrell "The Label Χριστιανός" 361–81. See also Holloway, *Coping with Prejudice*, 67.

51. Holloway, *Coping with Prejudice*, 71.

52. Holloway, *Coping with Prejudice*, 139

53. See the contrasting positions of David Balch, John Elliott, and Warren Carter.

that caution, psychological disidentification is an apt description of the counter-intuitive identity we have already highlighted. Moreover, identifying 1 Peter as a specialized form of the genre of consolation literature, opens up the possibility of appreciating in a new light the author's skillful use of Israel's scripture in providing support to a beleaguered community. We will return to these aspects later in the discussion.

Yet, Holloway's formulation of an answer to the driving question of the letter asks for more work to be done. The question of coping with prejudice actually begs a more fundamental question of the reliability of God as the basis for coping. Furthermore, the appeal to world-denying apocalyptic ideology cannot adequately account for notable aspects of the letter's attention to daily living such as: the careful advice given to the readers of 1 Peter about the particular demands of civic duty, how to manage the severe stress on relations between husbands and wives and between masters and slaves brought on by conversion, the exercise of common neighborliness, and everyday living within the community of faith. Volf comments on this relationship with the world in theological terms: "Christians are *insiders* who have diverted from their culture by being born again. They are by definition those who are not what they used to be, those who do not live like they used to live. Christian difference is therefore not an insertion of something new into the old from outside, but a bursting out of the new *precisely within the proper space of the old*."[54]

In addition, Seland observes, "1 Peter does not deal with the place of estrangement—that is, the world. The Christians' estrangement is not derived from their relations to the world. They are estranged to nonbelievers because of their relationship to God and their membership in the Christian community . . . . The estrangement seems to be perceived . . . more as a theological statement than as a social reality, though the latter is not completely excluded."[55] Clearly for Seland, the Christian deals principally with God who by causing their new birth creates estrangement.

Bechtler speaks of the addressees living in a situation of liminality. "Temporally, they find themselves to be participants in both the old aeon and the new simultaneously, yet not completely engaged in either; socially, they no longer participate fully in the institutions and lifestyle that defined

---

54. Volf, "Soft Difference," 18–19.

55. Seland, "πάροικος," 246. See also Feldmeier, *The First Letter of Peter*, 13, "So this description of being a foreigner does not lead to sectarian break with reality, but rather it opens up a new access to the surrounding world."

their lives prior to conversion, yet they have not withdrawn entirely from relations with their non-Christian neighbors."[56] He concludes, "Rather than encouraging hatred of the world, 1 Peter calls for a lifestyle that aims to win over the world; rather than hoping for retribution, 1 Peter hopes for the world's reconciliation (2:12; 3:1–2, 15–20) . . . . The strangers live out of God's future now opened to them by the death and resurrection of Christ; they can, therefore, be full of joy and hope even amid their suffering."[57]

This discussion displays again the tension between sectarian and accommodating options which characterize much of the discussion surrounding 1 Peter. What has become apparent is the need for an accounting of how the author of 1 Peter skillfully combines advice about caring for the life of the community in a world in which the readers live in some peril, *along with* anticipating their heavenly inheritance which will be brought to them upon the return of the resurrected Christ. My view is that the community's strong grasp on the faithfulness of God to adhere to God's commitments holds these two seemingly incompatible vectors in dynamic tension.

In sum, Holloway builds his case for seeing 1 Peter as a type of consolation literature cumulatively. While he can point to the technical language of consolation in 1 Pet 4:12, "Beloved, do not be surprised at the fiery ordeal that is taking place among you to test you, as though something strange were happening to you" the bulk of his argument is built by applying modern theories of coping (Disidentification, Behavioral Compensation, Attributional Ambiguity) to the exegesis of the text. However much there is to be gained from this exercise, I wish to bring into play evidence contained in the language of the letter which strengthens its description as consoling literature.

1 Peter and Israel's Consolation Scripture

It is well known that 1 Peter stands out among the writings of the New Testament for its extensive use of texts from the Old Testament to present its major themes.[58] Not only is the abundance of texts in such a short piece of Christian writing remarkable, but also the skillful interpretation of texts to illustrate its themes and to encourage belief. Isaiah is a principle source

---

56. Bechtler, *Following in His Steps*, 21.

57. Bechtler, *Following in His Steps*, 18.

58. See among others, Horrell, "Aliens and Strangers," 116–18, "The Themes of 1 Peter," and "'Race', 'Nation', 'People,'" 119, also Liebengood, *The Eschatology of 1 Peter*.

for these texts. The index of quotations in third edition of *The Greek New Testament* cites use of Isaiah seven times, mostly in 1 Pet 2. The canonical shape of Isaiah has long been recognized as a scripture meant to be heard as a word of encouragement to post-exilic Israel. [59] Isaiah was a natural source for the author of 1 Peter.

Another, less studied Old Testament source for 1 Peter's message of comfort is the Book of the Twelve.[60] While this terminology may be unfamiliar, it is fast gaining currency to describe the canonical shape of the collection Hosea through Malachi. For example, in 2011, Hanne von Weissenberg reported: "It is a general consensus of the scholarly community that the books of the Minor Prophets, and possibly the Twelve as a collection, had gained an elevated status as authoritative literature in the Second Temple period." He cited evidence from Qumran, the Murabba'at manuscript of the Minor Prophets and the Greek scroll from Nahal Hever.[61]

I am particularly interested in displaying the attractiveness of the Twelve to the author of 1 Peter who writes in order to encourage faith in its readers by demonstrating the faithfulness of God. One of the reasons someone writing a consolation epistle would turn to the Twelve is because it was already recognized as scripture of consolation. That this was the case can be demonstrated from two sources, Qumran and Sirach.

Von Weissenberg in a case study of the midrash of Amos 5:26–27 and 9:11 in the *Damascus Document* (CD A 7:13b–8:1a) concludes: "Whereas the . . . verse from the Book of Amos (5:7) announces the punishment of Israel's sins, the exile, in the *Damascus Document* the . . . prophecy is transformed into a 'positive message for the community, who wait for God's final judgement with eager anticipation.'"[62] This is consistent with maintaining the stamina of a sectarian community

Sirach is a book of late Wisdom literature, written early in the second century BCE. It eulogizes the Twelve specifically for its power to strengthen and support; "May the bones of the Twelve Prophets send forth new life from where they lie, for they comforted the people of Jacob and delivered them with confident hope" (Sir 49:10). We know from the prologue of this

---

59. See Childs, *Isaiah* and Seitz, *Zion's Final Destiny*.

60. Best, "1 Peter 2:4–10," 277–78, in 1969 noticed this relationship on the textual level.

61 *Changes in Scripture*, 248.

62. "The Twelve Minor Prophets," 370, referencing Grossman, *Reading for History*, 130, 160, 180, 197–98.

book that the writer's intention was to apply his "skill day and night to complete and publish the book for those living abroad who wished to gain learning and are disposed to live according to the law."[63] Thus the writer of Sirach recognized that the Twelve fit into his purpose to serve observant Jews living in diaspora by communicating comfort, hope, and instruction.[64] It is noteworthy that the only time Ben Sira uses the technical term *hakkātûb* ("the one about whom it is written") to introduce scripture in a formal way is in his citing the concluding verses of the Twelve, Mal 3:22–24 (LXX), in Sir 48:10 where the figure of Elijah is highlighted as the coming one "to restore the tribes of Judah."[65]

However, the possibility of using Sir 49:10 as evidence for the existence of the Twelve as authoritative literature in first century BCE remains an open question among some scholars. In 2015, von Weissenberg and Mika S. Pajunen observed that Sir 49:10 "gives no information on the order of the books, nor does it exclude the possibility that the books of this collection were copied separately."[66] After examining the fragments of the Twelve from Qumran (4QXII), they concluded that while a scroll containing books

---

63. Holloway, *Coping with Prejudice*, 95 cites the purpose of the Wisdom of Solomon, written most likely in the first century BCE "'to give comfort and encouragement' to the Jewish community in Alexandria, by assuring them that their God was the true power at work in the cosmos and that present injustices notwithstanding 'the souls of the righteous are in the hand of God', and 'their hope is full of immortality.'"

64. For evidence of the diasporitic setting of Sirach, see Gregory, "The Relationship between the Poor in Judea and Israel under Foreign Rule," 321, where in Sir 35:14–26 a transition occurs from the plight of the poor to the plight of Israel under foreign rule. Beentjes, "The Fluidity between the Oppressed of Israel and Israel the Oppressed, "66, points to Sir 35:17–19 where the plight of Israel is described as a homeless widow. In verse 35:17 a literal widow is meant, but in 35:18 the widow stands for the oppressed people of Israel. In Sir 35:19 the widow's homelessness is referenced. "Do not the tears of the widow run down her cheek as she cries out against her homelessness [the one who causes them to fall?]." Beentjes goes with the reading of Ms. B מרודיה and against a scribal error explanation for a putative "the one who made them [the tears] to fall." He also cites the two other uses of מרודיה in Lam 3:19 and Isa 58:7 for homelessness and the poor in the same semantic field. Thus the frequent mention of the poor and vulnerable in the Twelve are prime to being reinterpreted as referring to the plight of the nation in diaspora. Other late inter-testamental writings use similar analogies with the poor to refer to the diaspora. See The Sentences of Pseudo-Phocylides, 22–41, Sir 29:24–28, and Testament of Asher 7:1–7.

65. Koet, "Elijah as Reconciler of Father and Son," 183.

66. Pajunen and von Weissenberg, "The Book of Malachi," 733.

from the Twelve existed, reading the Twelve as a single, unified biblical book is a debatable issue.[67]

Despite this caution, clear evidence points to the Twelve being considered a single book by the time 1 Peter was written. As summarized by Marvin A. Sweeny:

> The first century C. E. Jewish historian Flavius Josephus apparently considers the Book of the Twelve as one of the twenty-two books of the Bible (*Against Apion* I. 8). Likewise, 4 Ezra 14:41 considers the Twelve to be one of the twenty-four holy books transcribed by Ezra . . . . The dual character of the book is evident in Talmudic tradition, which considers the Twelve as a single prophetic book that follows Isaiah, Jeremiah, and Ezekiel . . . and counts them as one book among the twenty-four of the Bible. But the Talmud also stipulates that whereas the books of the Bible are to be separated in manuscripts by four blank lines, the individual books of the Twelve Prophets are to be separated from each other by three blank lines . . . which indicates their dual status as separate books that nevertheless comprise a single book.[68]

Sirach uses the term "fear of the Lord" in 34:14-20 to stand for the comfort and deliverance through hope for which the Twelve Prophets are praised in inspiring diaspora Jews:

> The spirit of those who fear the Lord will live,
> for their hope is in him who saves them.
>
> Those who fear the Lord will not be timid,
> or play the coward, for he is their hope.
> Happy is the soul that fears the Lord!
> To whom does he look? And who is his support?
>
> The eyes of the Lord are on those who love him,
> a mighty shield and strong support,
> a shelter from scorching wind and a shade from noonday sun,
> a guard against stumbling and a help against falling.

Foremost in these verses is the divine initiative of salvation on which the believer throws everything for vindication. Images of divine faithfulness range from personal surveillance to impermeable barriers against mortal threats of both physical and natural origin, concluding with counter-measures which avoid costly mistakes (stumbling/falling). God's faithfulness supports

---

67. Von Weissenberg, "The Book of Malachi," 738.
68. Sweeny, *The Twelve Prophets*, xv–xvi.

a "fear of the Lord." This is a term of confessional orientation that amounts to a description of triumphant living consisting of utter dependence, confident expectation, steady courage, and lasting happiness.

Sirach shows that this profile of the interplay between divine faithfulness and human courage is the interpretative grid which guides readers toward what to look for in the Twelve. Perhaps one of the reasons the Twelve came in for such praise in Sirach is that this grid corresponds to the way the Twelve has been put together canonically. In the pages to follow, we will show how 1 Peter makes use of texts from the Book of the Twelve to press home the good news that God's prevenient faithfulness can be known within a beleaguered community of people who find themselves at odds with their familiar culture. Before embarking on this investigation, however, a brief summary of the canonical shape of the Twelve is in order. [69]

In an earlier study of the Twelve, I demonstrated that the final form of the Twelve stands as a scripture that portrays God undergirding Israel to withstand extreme pressures so as not to collapse into faithless despair.[70] This undergirding is played out through the motif of God's giving Israel the language it needs to speak in order to remain faithful to God.

These twelve disparate writings ranging from the eighth to the fourth centuries have been woven into a canonical document by means of a theological architecture that governs the ordering and interpretation of the document. This theological architecture has two systems. The first system is the *framing pieces*, Hosea and Malachi. They carry the twin emphases of: (1) the credibility of God's integrity proved by divine faithfulness and (2) the divine gift of the human capability to be faithful.[71] The framework announces the dominant message which will exercise an ordering rule within the variety of textual material. The dominant message operates to bring forward some texts of prominence while relegating other texts to a background role.[72] Between the two frames is the second system of *"load bearing members."* This system provides an internal cohesiveness as one reads across the rich texture of the books. The load bearing members are: (1)

---

69. For what follows, see Bailey, *Living in the Language*, 13–14.

70 See Bailey, *Living in the Language of God*, introduction and chapter 1.

71. In an important essay, "Another Look at the Hosea/Malachi Framework," Mark Leuchter recognizes the importance of the framework for setting the hermeneutical approach to the Twelve (ibid., 250).

72. Von Weissenberg, "The Twelve Minor Prophets," 367, has noticed how in the Qumran collection of the Twelve manuscripts, "not all of the books in an authoritative collection are necessarily authoritative in a similar way."

the formulae for divine self-designation (for example, Exod 34:6–7) which we will examine in chapter 2 and (2) the Day of the Lord events targeted toward the creation of faithful human speaking.[73]

Framing pieces and load bearing members become the skeleton of the Twelve which governs the interpretation of the whole. In other words, how texts function within the Book of the Twelve will turn upon the theological context set up around this skeleton which becomes the hermeneutical key to the body of the collection.[74] As Seitz explains: "a canonical reading... works with one cardinal rule: it seeks to pay attention to what the canonical form has itself given priority to, and also what not. That is, it judges the final form as itself a proper commentary on its history of development, wherein certain features are foregrounded and others are left in the background."[75]

In sum, the theological shaping of the Twelve delivers a message that resonates with Sirach's interpretative grid of what to look for in the Twelve for those who live in some state of alienation in the last two centuries BCE. We now turn to the Twelve's contribution to the desire of 1 Peter to encourage and to bring consolation to Christians of the first century CE.

---

73 This way of interpreting the Twelve resonates with findings of the newer form criticism of the Twelve. See Stovell, "'I Will Make Her Like a Desert,'" 46, who reminds that "Genre does not exist separately from linguistic contexts, but is always contextualized by linguistic frameworks that provide clarity on genre's meaning in a given passage. Recent shifts in genre analysis have started to acknowledge the need for linguistic contextualization as a necessary part of genre theory."

74. Sweeney, *The Twelve Prophets*, I, xxvi, cautions against a "relatively mechanical association of catchwords" as being sufficient to establish an intentional uniting of the constituent books of the Twelve. However, he does recognize that "many intertextual citations among the Twelve... do point to interrelationships that must be evaluated." In his analysis of the reception of the Twelve, Ben Zvi, "Twelve Prophetic Books," 149–54 sets out the alternatives as either a *reception-centered approach* that emphasizes the role of the reader to create interrelationships between twelve separate books or a *production-centered approach* which emphasizes the role of the author(s) in crafting a single document. My position is based in a production-centered approach.

75. Seitz, *Joel*, 13. Nogalski notes that the violence of Nahum toward the nations "should not simply be accepted [theologically] in our day." "Reading the Book of the Twelve Theologically," 118.

2

The Contribution of the Twelve to the Message of Consolation in 1 Peter

Orientation to the Investigation

1. Hermeneutical Assumptions

FIRST PETER 1:10–12 STATES that the message of consolation is already within the canon of scripture and available to the churches of Anatolia, specifically the division of the Hebrew Bible called the Prophets: these verses lay down an exegetical foundation for the epistle's use of scripture.[1]

> Concerning this salvation, the prophets who prophesized of the grace that was to be yours made careful search and inquiry, inquiring about the person or time that the Spirit of Christ within them indicated when it testified in advance to the sufferings destined for Christ and the subsequent glory. It was revealed to them that they were serving not themselves but you, in regard to the things that have now been announced to you through those who brought you good news by the Holy Spirit sent from heaven—things into which angels long to look!

---

1. Horrell, "Jesus Remembered in 1 Peter?" 148, identifies 1 Pet 1:10–12 as the hermeneutical foundation for the author's use of the Old Testament. For earlier investigation of this crucial text, see Schutter, *Hermeneutic and Composition*, 85–109. Schutter contends that the epistle was written as an emergency pastoral letter to a circle of churches experiencing a crisis of localized persecution. The theme of the contrast between sufferings and consummation, which he believes is the result of the exegesis of the prophets, becomes for him a kind of schema which helps to organize Old Testament references throughout the letter. Thus the interplay between suffering and future glory informs his description of 1:13—2:10 as an exhortation to readers under fiery trials, after the manner of Jewish homiletic midrash, to be holy as the Lord is holy.

It is worth noting that the announcers of good news, including the writer of the epistle, found the content of their proclamation ready to hand in what the prophets had already set down. They understood that the ancient prophets were directly serving them. Hermeneutically, we can construe this to mean that these first-century Christians perceived that the way they listened to the text was the way Isaiah and the Twelve did so as well. Or, in other words, 1 Peter's interpretative grid, which was keyed to bring comfort based upon the prevenient faithfulness of God, was compatible with what Isaiah and the Twelve were doing. Therefore, from the vantage point of the epistle, the prophets can be said to have been serving those who announced good news to the Anatolians.

This overlapping of hermeneutical grids had precedent. As has already been noted, Sirach praises the prophets who make up the Twelve for serving Jews in second century BCE with comfort and strength. Sirach's endorsement is informed by his finding a match between his hermeneutical grid, which is the interplay between divine faithfulness and human courage, and the way the Twelve has been put together as a scripture that undergirds the credibility of God and the capability of Israel.[2] Even those who put together the canonical form of the Twelve itself, made the individual writings "serve" the historical context at the time of their shaping.[3]

The author of 1 Peter identifies the Spirit of Christ speaking within the Old Testament prophets of his prospective sufferings and subsequent glory. Only from a position of looking backward from the time and setting of the epistle can one perceive that the Hebrew prophets of the eighth through the fourth century BCE engaged in a program of concentrated investigating and searching diligently[4] to discern the sufferings of Christ and his subsequent glory. First-century Christian prophets believed that they shared the same (Holy) Spirit who inspires older scripture to be heard and re-appropriated as Christian scripture in new situations to achieve similar

---

2. See Bailey, *Living in the Language of God*.

3 See the fundamental work of Childs, "Retrospective Reading," 377: "these writings function as Scripture for someone. They have been ordered toward a present and future audience who receives its identity in some way from Israel's past story which is lost if a new story is reconstructed apart from the received narrative form." See also Seitz, "On Letting a Text 'Act Like a Man,'" 167 "the heart of canonical reading . . . is . . . that aspect of God's word to Israel which continues to press for a hearing and addresses new generations with an old word, borne of a specific time and specific application, and without shedding that, moving forward through time to enclose new readers and new situations."

4 The verbs ἐξεζήτησαν and ἐηραὔνησαν convey a sense of urgency.

outcomes of faithfulness.⁵ What makes this coordination between first century and previous prophetic exegesis productive and meaningful is the sharing of an interpretative grid of similar theological character.⁶

2. Textual and Literary Considerations

The consolation of 1 Peter consists of displaying the undergirding faithfulness of God to protect the loyalty of believers against various trials which redounds to the praise, honor, and glory of God when Christ is revealed (1 Pet 1:5–7). God's undergirding faithfulness permits believers to remain faithful under duress and to conduct their lives on the basis of the evidence of Jesus that is impervious to physical influence, thus protecting their salvation (1 Pet 1:8–9). The overall character of 1 Peter's consolation is positive and hopeful, while remaining soberly realistic.

This consolation is targeted to the driving question of the letter: Given the experience of suffering because one is charged with the offense of being a Christian, will God be faithful in vindicating the Christian's confession of loyalty to Jesus Christ? Can God be trusted to uphold Christians in their being tried by torture and even death? Does the Christian have to worry about being "put to shame" by God's abandonment in the hour of greatest need?

The aim of this chapter is to make plain how the Book of the Twelve aids this epistle in answering these questions in order to give good counsel and comfort. Critically, it will be necessary to adjudicate literary matters of whether a text in 1 Peter refers to a citation from or an allusion to the Twelve. If it is a citation, is its source the Hebrew or Greek version? Where are the

---

5. Horrell, "Jesus Remembered in 1 Peter?" 144, asks the question: What drove the author of 1 Peter to the selection of certain passages or traditions? "This is not prophecy historicized (a la Crossin) where the story is more or less fabricated by engagement with Scripture. This is history prophetically explained." See also Childs, "Retrospective Reading," 373 "history is understood in the light of prophecy, not prophecy in the light of history." And Seitz, "On Letting a Text 'Act Like a Man,'" 168: "The very notion of a canonical process assumes a doctrine of inspiration that spills out from the prophetic word once delivered, as God superintends that word toward his own accomplishing end . . . . The original word pressing forward towards a horizon God alone means to illumine, with recourse to that original word of his own, divulged by the work of the Holy Spirit in a new day."

6. Childs, "Retrospective Reading," 373, "there are characteristic ways in which the prophets were edited, not simply in terms of particular literary techniques, but through a theological stance toward the material which has deeply affected the transmission process throughout the oral, written, and redactional stages."

critical departures from the source text? If it is an allusion, is it of primary or secondary nature (that is, is the allusion tied directly to the Twelve or is it awakened by a citation from another text of the Hebrew Bible)?[7]

Finally, the contribution of the Twelve to the interpretative punch of the text in 1 Peter will be described as precisely as possible. In evaluating this contribution terms such as covert or invisible midrash or the technique of *gezerah shavah* may be used to describe the work of the author of 1 Peter. Covert midrash covers the process of interpreting a religious idea from a given text without the text or midrashic technique being named, defined, or mentioned.[8] The technique of *gezerah shavah* is the interpretation of a text in light of another text via a related word or phrase.[9]

The use of these techniques awakens a range of texts in the reader's world, and draws readers to imagine how similar themes or narratives mutually interpret one another.[10] As Dryden explains,

> the author only refers to key elements of the story of salvation to evoke an entire narrative worldview that is familiar to both author and readers. This sort of shorthand description of key elements is, as we have noted before, typical of paraenesis, where only a few key points need to be reviewed and emphasized. Thus, what we have access to in the epistle is that portion of the entire presupposed narrative theological worldview that the author found it useful to highlight. The author's goal is to be relevant not comprehensive.[11]

The Conversation between 1 Peter and the Twelve

While every chapter of 1 Peter has been influenced by the Septuagint, the highest concentration of citations and allusions appear in the first two

---

7. See further, Ben-Porat, "The Poetics of Literary Allusions," 107–8, quoted by Liebengood, *The Eschatology of 1 Peter*, 14.

8. Gertner, "Midrashim in the New Testament," 268, quoted in Liebengood, *The Eschatology of 1 Peter*, 96.

9. Liebengood, *The Eschatology of 1 Peter*, 95.

10. Liebengood, *The Eschatology of 1 Peter*, 103.

11. Dryden, *Theology and Ethics in 1 Peter*, 66, quoted by Liebengood, *The Eschatology of 1 Peter*, 201. See also Ben-Porat, "The Poetics of Literary Allusions," 107–8. The reader activates the evoked text as a whole in an attempt to form connections between the alluding text and the evoked text. Schuitter, *Hermeneutic and Composition*, 94–95, describes how in the tradition of Synagogue preaching specific Old Testament texts may associate themselves with entire blocks of text.

chapters. Feldmeier points out that "Only in Hebrews and the Apocalypse do we find a comparable density of the Old Testament citations and allusions. With two exceptions [1:16 and 2:6] texts are not specially designated (it is written etc.) . . . . [T]he language of the biblical Scriptures merges as it were organically into the exposition of the letter and proves to be a decisive reference point and foundation for this argumentation."[12] The remainder of this chapter investigates the author's use of texts in the Twelve as a book of comfort in order to craft a message of consolation that emphasizes the faithfulness of God undergirding human loyalty in the face of testing.

1. Being Born Anew, 1 Peter 1:3–5

> Blessed be the God and Father of our Lord Jesus Christ! By his great mercy he has given us a new birth into a living hope through the resurrection of Jesus Christ from the dead, and into an inheritance that is imperishable, undefiled, and unfading, kept in heaven for you, who are being protected by the power of God through [God's] faithfulness for a salvation ready to be revealed in the last time.

The writer of 1 Peter would have been familiar with the concept of being born anew since it was used by Philo and Judaic proselyte literature as well as the Greek Mysteries in their description of conversion to indicate a "decisively new stage in nature, history or personal life."[13] As has already been noted in chapter 1, Peter employs the figure of speech "born again" in two different ways. In 1:3 the act of being born anew is attributed broadly to the mercy of God. The orientation of this new birth is to a personal, living hope underwritten by the death-defying resurrection of Jesus. In 1:23 the new birth is attributed instrumentally to the imperishable word of God, which comes in the form of the preached good news. The orientation of new birth is toward one's behavior in the community of believers. In both instances, the writer places heavy emphasis on the unshakable faithfulness of God which buttresses the solidity of the believer's new birth. The following discussion will take up both aspects of new birth, personal and communal.

The concept of new birth as such does not appear in the Old Testament. Nevertheless, Horrell presents evidence that ties the prophecy of

---

12. Feldmeier, *The First Letter of Peter*, 26.

13. Selwyn, *The First Epistle of St. Peter*, 122. See Feldmeier, *The First Letter of Peter*, 127–29.

Jonah within the Book of the Twelve to 1 Peter through this very theme.[14] This evidence is strong enough to establish a presumption for Jonah's role in shaping the concept of new birth in the epistle.[15] Horrell draws attention to the collocation of Jonah and 1 Peter in the Crosby-Schøyen Codex (C-S) found in the early Christian library of the Pacomian monastic Order in Upper Egypt discovered late in 1952 near Dishnā. Written in Sahidic Coptic, the Greek Vorlage on which C-S depends existed perhaps as early as late second century.[16]

The Codex contains: Melito of Sardis *On the Passover*; 2 Macc 5:27—7:41; 1 Peter; Jonah, and an unidentified text (pagination missing). According to Charles Hedrick, editor and translator of the C-S text of Jonah, "The relatively numerous remains of the Coptic text of Jonah suggest that it played a significant role in the liturgical life of early Coptic Christianity particularly in Upper Egypt."[17] Among the reasons why the text of Jonah may have appealed to readers who also treasured 1 Peter is its analogy to the resurrection of Jesus. The ejection of Jonah after three days in the belly of the whale is a kind of new birth and as such typified the new birth of hope the readers of 1 Peter experienced through the preaching of the resurrection of Jesus.[18] Jonah's turning to God in the belly of the fish and his subsequent ejection was also exploited by Hellenistic Diaspora Judaism in Ps. Philo" *De Jonah* sec. 95. 99 to describe the new birth of proselytes. This prompts further investigation into a possible relationship between Jonah and 1 Peter.

14. Horrell, "The Themes of 1 Peter," 502–22.

15. Horrell, "The Themes of 1 Peter," 522, states cautiously, "In identifying ... themes as central to the letter, these codices—products and reflections of a somewhat later time and context—do not, of course, allow us to assume that these were also in the mind of the author of 1 Peter. But they do provide a view, an interpretation of the letter, which can, not entirely unlike exegetical works and commentaries (also reflections of later times and contexts), point us to the theological centre of the letter and to its dominant themes and concerns—whether or not these were consciously intended by its author."

16. Horrell, "The Themes of 1 Peter," 503–4. William Willis, editor and translator of the text of 1 Peter in the Codex concludes "that it may be dated with some confidence to the middle of the III century" (Willis, "Letter of Peter (1 Peter)," *Crosby-Schøyen Codex*, 137).

17. Hedrick, "Jonah the Prophet (Jonah)," 507.

18. Jonah will figure significantly again in 1 Peter's treatment of Jesus in 3:21–23. Horrell brings together other reasons to explain Jonah's collocation with 1 Peter in the C-S Codex. Among them are: Jonah's prayer to God in the midst of his affliction (2:2–9) is especially apposite for those who are suffering affliction, even to death, or who look to God as the source of their salvation, and the missionary witness of God's people in a hostile world and their hope for vindication and salvation.

The theme of new birth complies well with the position that its addressees have found themselves in—exiles and aliens to their culture precisely because of their being born anew into an existence defined by the resurrection of Jesus.[19] Their new birth occurs in 1 Peter in texts that call out the faithfulness of God as the foundation for the steadiness of the believer. Those born anew are being preserved by the power of God through God's faithfulness (1:5), and similarly God sires those born anew from a word that stands forever (1:25). Jonah has a peculiar role to play within the Twelve in enunciating the reliability of God's merciful love as the efficient cause of the believer's conversion and preservation. A brief discussion of this theme in Jonah within the context of the Twelve will make its association with 1 Peter clearer.

As was described at the conclusion of chapter 1, the creation of the Twelve involved ordering the disparate writings between the two bookends, Hosea and Malachi, with their twin emphases of the divine credibility undergirding human capability. These fundamental conceptions are coordinated with two themes which run through the collection of (1) the exploration of the formula for divine self-disclosure and (2) the Day of the Lord as the occasion for the creation of human speech. Both themes are appropriated in 1 Peter through the imagery of being born anew. Jonah plays a crucial role in the development of the first theme of divine self-disclosure. In the next section we will show how Hos 2:21–23 undergirds 1 Peter's use of the second theme.

To summarize what I have previously written in greater detail,[20] the base-text for the formula of divine self-disclosure is Exod 34:6–7. [21]

> The LORD, the LORD,
>
> a God merciful and gracious,
>
> slow to anger,
>
> and abounding in steadfast love and faithfulness,
>
> keeping steadfast love for the thousandth generation,
>
> forgiving iniquity and transgression and sin,
>
> yet by no means clearing the guilty,
>
> but visiting the iniquity of the parents

---

19. See among others, Horrell, "Aliens and Strangers," 116, 131; "Between Conformity," 116; Seland, "πάροικος," 245, 248, 254; and Volf, "Soft Difference," 17–18.

20. Bailey, *Living in the Language of God*, 36–40.

21. Bailey, *The Self-Shaming God*, 60–65.

> upon the children
>
> and the children's children,
>
> to the third and the fourth generation.

This self-designation formula of the bi-focal sovereignty of God shows up most clearly in Mic 7:18–20 which brings that book to a climactic end and in Nah 1:2–3a.

> Who is a God like you, pardoning iniquity
>
> and passing over the transgression
>
> of the remnant of your possession?
>
> He does not retain his anger forever,
>
> because he delights in showing clemency.
>
> He will again have compassion upon us;
>
> he will tread our iniquities under foot.
>
> You will cast all our sins
>
> into the depths of the sea.
>
> You will show faithfulness to Jacob
>
> and unswerving loyalty to Abraham,
>
> as you have sworn to our ancestors
>
> from the days of old.
>
> A jealous and avenging God is the Lord,
>
> the Lord is avenging and wrathful,
>
> the Lord takes vengeance on his adversaries
>
> and rages against his enemies.
>
> The Lord is slow to anger but great in power,
>
> and the Lord will by no means clear the guilty.

In the Hebrew Bible, the juncture of Micah and Nahum at the midpoint of the Book of the Twelve secures its key-stone position of the collection. The double statement of God's mercy and judgment thus provides the pivot point around which the separate writings of the collection are turned into a coherent theological statement of God's bi-focal sovereignty.[22]

In the LXX ordering, Micah is separated from Nahum, apparently from a desire to group together the prophets of the eighth century (Hosea, Amos and Micah). However, the books that follow these three (Joel, Obadiah,

---

22. Bailey, *Self-Shaming God*, 60–61.

Jonah, Nahum) preserve the original theological statement of God's mercy and judgment (Jonah 4:2b and Nah 1:2b–3).[23] Thus, this statement retains its pivotal hermeneutical place at the mid-point of the Twelve.

In the fifteen instances where this self-designation formula is quoted in the Old Testament, five occur in the Book of the Twelve. In addition to the exuberant praise and sobering warning of Micah and Nahum, the formula figures heavily in God's statement to take Israel as wife "in righteousness and in justice, in steadfast love, and in mercy . . . in faithfulness; and you shall know the Lord (Hos 2:19–20 [Eng]). It motivates a liturgy of repentance in Joel 2:12–14: "Return to the Lord, your God, for he is gracious and merciful, slow to anger, and abounding in steadfast love, and relents of punishing. Who knows whether he will not turn and relent, and leave a blessing behind him?"

Jonah parodies this theological statement in his assault on God's integrity for sparing Nineveh: "for I knew that you are a gracious God and merciful, slow to anger, and abounding in steadfast love, and ready to relent from punishing" (4:2) This parody underscores the how crucial the confession of God's faithfulness is to the framers of the Twelve.

This definition of the Being of God in God's acts of love and justice has the character of a standing formula and a liturgical doxology. It is a major part of the architecture of the Twelve where it functions as the hermeneutical horizon to understand the message of the Twelve.[24] By 1 Peter's referencing those newly converted as being "born anew" the writer is activating a rich and complex symbol world for his readers, and on the basis of the C-S codex Jonah has a prominent place in that symbol world. Jonah places the formula of God's faithfulness on the lips of one born anew from the belly of a fish, even if his speech is in the form of a parody of that confession. This gives indisputable weight to the divine faithfulness undergirding those who have been born anew by the gospel. In sum, the story of Jonah may

---

23. See a paper presented to the Southwest Commission on Religious Studies, March 14, 2014, by Roy E. Garton. He argues that there was a pre-cursor Book of the Four consisting of Obadiah-Jonah-Nahum-Habakkuk. If this is so, then the framers of the Hebrew Book of the Twelve have blurred the focus on Assyria by separating Jonah and Nahum with the insertion of Micah and its concern for the integrity of God ("Where is your God?") in Mic 7:1–10. Garton's position would seem to support the theory that the pre-cursor collection, Obad-Hab, would have remained at hand to be employed in the LXX. Would that arrangement's emphasis on the sovereignty of God in the context of a focus on Assyria have resonated, as a source of comfort, with Israel's life under foreign domination?

24. Miskotte, *When the Gods Are Silent*, 193.

be appreciated as a sub-text for 1 Peter's use of the imagery of being born anew. The pairing of Jonah with 1 Peter in the C-S Codex suggests strongly Jonah's role as a commentary on the epistle. The reliability of God's living up to God's Name could receive no better confirmation than the confession of the "born anew" Jonah.

2. Sired by the Word, 1 Peter 1:23

> You have been born anew, not of perishable but of imperishable seed, through the living and enduring word of God (or, through the word of the living and enduring God).

The foregoing discussion has secured the assertion that a new birth defines the addressees of the letter. The centrality of this assertion is supported by its reappearance in 1 Pet 1:23, where it is amplified by the thought of being born into a living hope through being sired by the imperishable word of God. Because of that new birth and parentage, the addressees have withdrawn from former habits and associations, prompting their being accused of being Christian. They have become aliens and sojourners in a native environment wherein they encounter a threat which is likely to become hostile.[25] The author engages this threat through emphasizing that nothing can shake the substance of their new birth. First Peter 1:24–25 calls upon an important text from Isa 40:6–8 to anchor within God's character the lasting quality of being sired by God's word:

> "All flesh is like grass
> and all its glory like the flower of grass.
> The grass withers,
> and the flower falls,
> but the word of the LORD endures forever."
> That word is the good news that was announced to you.

In his commentary, Feldmeier makes an insightful observation about the effect of being born anew through the word: "Rebirth stresses that the new existence is thanks to the God who in his word *gives us participation*

---

25. For access to the wide discussion of these terms, see Horrell, "Aliens and Strangers," 116, 131; "'Race', 'Nation', 'People,'" 156 and "Between Conformity," 127.

in himself. Through the new siring, God *grants participation in his own livingness and eternity.*"[26]

We have already noted that the idea of being born anew has little traction in the Old Testament. However, the notion of God's giving God's word as a pathway to participating in God's "livingness and eternity" is frequently encountered. This is the second theme noted earlier which is associated with the canonical shaping of the Twelve where God either prompts faithful speech or puts words of faithfulness into speakers' mouths. The life-giving effects of participation in God's word give comfort in the Twelve. First Peter 2:10 draws upon this in a quotation which is a composite of Hos 1:6, 9; 2:23.[27]

> Once you were not a people,
> but now you are God's people;
> once you had not received mercy,
> but now you have received mercy.

Hosea 2:21–23 is the base text which the author of 1 Peter has shaped:

> On that day . . . I will have pity on Lo-ruhamah, [Not Pitied]
> and I will say to Lo-ammi [Not My People] "You are my people";
> and he shall say, "You are my God."

This solemn declaration from God has the effect of reversing identities of judgment and rejection, and puts words of covenant loyalty into the mouth of Israel. The result is that God's people may live in a new identity, and God may enjoy covenantal fellowship with God's people. This declaration in Hosea caps a series of language-swaps where God takes words out of the mouths of God's people and replaces them with words that enable what God wants for God's people. For example, Hos 2:16–17 (Heb 2:18–19).[28] "On that day, says the LORD, you will call me, 'My husband,' and no longer will you call me, 'My Baal.' For I will remove the names of the Baals from her mouth, and they shall be mentioned by name no more." This is a re-statement of the covenantal dictum "I will take you as my people, and I will be your God" (Exod 6:7). The direct intervention by God re-constitutes a people by giving it new words to speak, much as in Hos 14:2–3, God gives Israel words to say that provide a pathway for God to heal them.

---

26. Feldmeier, *The First Letter of Peter*, 130 (emphasis added).
27. Exod 19:5–6 also may figure here as well as in 2:9.
28. Bailey, *Living in the Language of God*, 57–59, 139 for other examples.

Of special note is that the reconstituting of identity through the re-birth of language happens in the context of "in that day." This is the standard shorthand allusion to the Day of the LORD which occurs throughout prophetic literature with heavy concentrations in the Book of the Twelve.[29] One of the more significant results of the inbreaking of the Day in the Twelve is God's creating and giving words for humans to speak as their pathway to their new identity of being in covenant relationship with God. God proves God's faithful commitment to love God's people by giving God's people their language of faithfulness. For example, in Zeph 3:14–18

> Sing aloud, O daughter Zion;
>
> shout, O Israel!
>
> Rejoice and exult with all your heart,
>
> O daughter Jerusalem! . . .
>
> The LORD, your God, is in your midst,
>
> a warrior who gives victory;
>
> he will rejoice over you with gladness,
>
> he will renew you in his love;
>
> he will exult over you with loud singing
>
> as on a day of festival.

Thus, the invitation to Zion to "*Sing* aloud . . . . *Rejoice and exult* with all your heart" (Zeph 3:14) can be issued in all confidence because "The LORD . . . will *rejoice* over you with gladness . . . he will *exult* over you with loud *singing*" (3:17b). Because God creates speech, human words are taken up into God's language of renewal in divine love. "At the level of experience, and caught up in the ordering of the words, God's joy and shout, and Israel's joy and shout, qualify and amplify each other."[30] God evokes the special energy of language, rooted deep in the human consciousness, to seal the promise of restoration.[31]

In Hosea, God creates a new people by giving them new covenantal language to speak. The author of 1 Pet 2:10 turns Israel's covenantal language into the word for proclaimers to announce. The force of this adaptation

---

29 Bailey, *Living in the Language of God*, 41.

30 McEvenue, "The Truth Trap," 182.

31 Albertz, "Exile as Purification," 223, notes the redactional character of Zeph 3:14–20, identifying it as the work of those who put together Hosea, Amos, Micah, and Zephaniah as the Book of the Four, a putative precursor to the Twelve.

is felt both retrospectively and immediately. Retrospectively, the solemn pronouncement, "Once . . . now; once . . . now," harks back to 1 Pet 1:23 and becomes the content of the word of the Lord which sires being born anew. This is the word that "endures forever . . . the good news that was announced to you" (1:25). However, in the immediate context of 2:9, "Once . . . now; once . . . now" becomes the word of proclamation placed in the speech of the "chosen race, royal priesthood, holy nation, Gods own people [literally, a people for his possession]."[32] The listeners to the proclamation of the good news are born anew by the power of the message of the resurrection. This event aligns 1 Peter with the perspective of the Book of the Twelve where Israel is re-constituted as God's covenantal people when they receive new language "in that day."

3. A People for His Possession, 1 Peter 2:9

> But you are a chosen race, a royal priesthood, a holy nation, God's own people [Gk. a people for his possession], in order that you may proclaim the mighty acts of him who called you out of darkness into his marvelous light.

In Horrell's investigation of race, priesthood, nation, and people[33] he describes how these fundamental terms helped to solidify Jewish identity within the Hellenistic world. He models his discussion on what Eberhard Schwarz observed of how identity was maintained through distinction *(Abgrenzung)* in the book of Jubilees. Schwarz "identifies three fundamental identity-forming designations *(Identitatsgrundende Assagen)* of Israel: Israel as 'holy people', Israel as 'chosen people' and Israel as a people who belong to God, God's special possession *(Eigentumsvolk)*. It is striking that all three of these designations are repeated in 1 Pet 2:9."[34]

    An important aspect of these identity-forming designations is that they are "*social constructions*, the product of specific historical and geographical

---

32. The author is making use of a literary feature called "embedded speech" which occurs frequently in the Book of the Twelve. The feature functions to convey the action of God authenticating divine faithfulness by giving God's people the ability to show through speech their capability to live in covenant with God. See Bailey, *Living in the Language of God.*

33 Horrell, "'Race', 'Nation', 'People,'" 131–63.

34. Horrell, "'Race', 'Nation', 'People,'" 139, referencing Schwarz, *Identitat durch Abgrenzungsprozesse in Israel,* 53–7.

forces, rather than biologically given ideas whose meaning is dictated by nature."[35] Horrell draws further upon the work of Hall and Brett to add that these social constructions of identity are ultimately constructed through written and spoken discourse and as such identity has to be maintained by reiterated practices and discursive strategies.[36] Ethnic identity is something believed and confessed rather than something objective or factual.[37] Such observations are salient in understanding how early Christians living around the Mediterranean basin could be addressed as a race, priesthood, nation, and people.

These designations awaken important texts in the Hebrew Bible for 1 Peter which Horrell identifies as informing the author's four-fold characterization of his addressees.[38] Exodus 19:5–6 echo the first three terms; Isa 43:20 describes Israel as "my chosen people"; and Isa 43:21 adds that the mission of this people is "to declare my praise."

However, as we look at how the Book of the Twelve aided the writer of this epistle to frame his message of consolation, the final term in this series has particular relevance. What is of particular interest is the author's choice of the nominal phrase εἰς περιποίησιν to describe "a people for his possession." This precise phrase occurs in Mal 3:17 where God uses it to declare divine commitment to God's people who, despite being put to shame by the unchecked perfidy of compatriots, yet stand up to temptation to renounce their loyalty God (3:14).[39] Thus, both Isaiah and Malachi are sources for this particular term of how those sired by the word are to call themselves.[40] Yet, the circumstances of struggle with doubt which surrounds Malachi's use urges us to focus on its comparability to the situation of the readers of 1 Peter. Moreover, as we will demonstrate shortly, in the prophet's larger encouragement to those who are made to feel ashamed of their loyalty, Mal 3:16–18 finds a new hearing in the epistle.

---

35. Jackson and Penrose, "Introduction: Placing 'Race' and 'Nation,'" 1. Quoted by Feldmeier, *The Letter of 1 Peter*, 17.

36. Horrell, "'Race', 'Nation', 'People'," 158, quoting from Hall, *Ethnic Identity*, 2, 41 and Brett, "Interpreting Ethnicity," 10. See chapter 3 for the emphasis in 1 Peter on worship as the context for identity formation and also Bailey, *Living in the Language of God*, 127–28.

37. Bailey, *Living in the Language of God*, 161.

38. Bailey, *Living in the Language of God*, 140.

39. Bauckham, "James, 1 and 2 Peter, Jude," 311, argues that the base text is Exod 19:5 even though "sĕgullā . . . translated λαὸς περιούσιος in Exod. 19:5 LXX."

40. Schutter, *Hermeneutic and Composition*, 40.

We note that Isaiah and Malachi each contribute a unique aspect to what it means to be God's special possession. Drawing from Isa 43:21 (LXX "my people whom I have procured to exposit my virtues"), they are "to proclaim the virtues of the one who called you out of darkness into his marvelous light." Seland points to the likelihood that the epistle writer has likely augmented the source text by "the particular diaspora Jewish ways of describing the transition made by Gentiles when they converted to Judaism."[41] Philo, for example, says concerning the proselytes that "we must rejoice with them, as if, though blind at the first, they had recovered their sight and had come from the deepest darkness to behold the most radiant light."[42] Thus, this final term in 1 Peter's series, describing the vocation of proclamation for the addressees, has their status as proselytes in view, and the entire series honors them in that status.

This honoring takes on further weight in the light of the epistle's frank recognition that those who have become proselytes have rendered themselves liable for "fiery trails" (2:11–12). This, too, was supported by Jewish experience, as Bergen explains: "According to Philo, conversion meant that the proselytes made a sociological, judicial and ethnic break with pagan society and joined another ethnic group, the Jewish nation"[43] at the risk of their lives.

In Mal 3:17 God's people are pointed out as God's special possession because they are remaining faithful under severe stress. Malachi 3:13–17 describes God's people so doubting God's credibility they are ready to give up the disciplines that shape their lives as God's people. "It is vain to serve God. What do we profit by keeping his command or by going about as mourners before the LORD of hosts? Now we count the arrogant happy; evildoers not only prosper, but when they put God to the test they escape." Facing down this threat, "those who revered the LORD" continued to shape their lives by engaging in liturgical acts centered on the speaking of God's name ("a book of remembrance was written before [the LORD] for those

---

41. Seland, "πάροικος," 259–60

42. In the novel *Joseph and Aseneth* (100 BCE–100 CE) Joseph in his prayer for Aseneth (8:9–10) says "Lord God of my father Israel, the Powerful One of Jacob, who gave life to all (things) and called (them) from the darkness to the light and from error to truth, and from the death to life."

43 Borgen, "The Early Church", 213. "The Early Church draws on traditions, debates and practices from Jewish proselytism, modifies them, and makes them to serve a different kind of community structure." 208. Cited by Seland, "πάροικος," 241 and 262.

who revered the Lord and thought on his name").[44] It is this community of faithful speakers who struggle in the midst of severe testing that God calls "my special possession" and promises the relief of a grateful parent. Thus the epistle borrows from the witness of the struggles in Malachi to enrich its message of encouragement.

By the skillful combination of resources in Isaiah and Malachi, the author of 1 Peter reminds his readers simultaneously of their status as honored proselytes and their vocation to engage in liturgical rehearsal of the good news. 1 Peter uses scripture to describe the church in terms of its status and vocation.[45] Moreover, by placing the paraphrase from Hosea, "Once . . . now, once . . . now," as the climatic conclusion to this peroration of God's people, the author effectively gestures to the opening and closing books of the Twelve and brackets this major source alongside Isaiah as being determinative for the comfort the letter offers. "Once . . . now; once . . . now" becomes the word of proclamation from the "chosen race, royal priesthood, holy nation, Gods own people [literally, a people for his possession]" who are being strengthened to remain faithful in their trials. Their proclaimed word is the summation of "the mighty acts of him who called you out of darkness into his marvelous light."

Thus it is possible to describe 1 Pet 1:3–2:10 as the opening theological section which states the new existence of the readers as being born anew into a living hope and rivets their rebirth into the preaching of the word of the life, death, and resurrection of Jesus. By our participation in God's preached word, the good news of the resurrection of a crucified Jesus is born in us as our living hope. The word is preached as the occasion for the creation of the living hope necessary for coping with this life.

4. Jesus and Shame, 1 Peter 2:6

For it stands in scripture:

See, I am laying in Zion a stone,

A cornerstone chosen and precious,

And whoever believes in him will not be put to shame.

---

44. For exegetical development of this text see Bailey, *Living in the Language*, 67–75, 82.

45. Horrell, "Jesus Remembered," 148, calls this "the scripturalization of an ecclesiastical reality."

Centered within the framework of new birth are complementary ways the metaphor of Jesus as God's stone are developed. In the first instance, Jesus is the living stone, actually the living keystone around which the living stones of believers are built into a spiritual house.[46] This spiritual house is actually a temple wherein the living stones are to act as holy priests offering a sacrificial worship pleasing to God through Jesus Christ (1 Pet 2:4–5). The liturgical activity of God's people in this extended metaphor has many points of contact with the series of terms that apply to God's people born anew: (chosen race, kingdom of priests, holy nation, a people for God's possession, proclaimers of mighty acts). The author of the epistle cites in 2:6 the root of this extended metaphor as Isa 28:16 LXX which the author applies directly to Jesus.

> Because of this, thus says the Lord:
>
> Behold I am laying in Zion a stone, expensive and chosen, a cornerstone, highly valued
>
> into her foundations

The final line of this text provides the epistle's author with the second application of the stone metaphor to Jesus "and whoever believes/trusts in him/it will not be put to shame."[47] As the subsequent citation of Ps 118:33 in 2:7 indicates, not being put to shame is equivalent to not stumbling and falling which are common descriptions of the collapse of faith and loyalty.[48] The one who trusts in Jesus will not collapse.

Before considering this crucial assertion, it will be helpful to be reminded that in chapter 1 we drew from both the letter itself ("However, if you suffer as a Christian, do not be ashamed, but praise God that you bear that name," 4:16) and from the insightful letter of Pliny to Trajan to show that shame in the form of public exposure, ridicule, humiliation, torture, and execution were very real possibilities in the fiery trials that lay in store for those to whom 1 Peter was directed. A new birth into a living hope brought with it this terrifying liability. Shame in the form of abandonment, vulnerability, assault, insult, and trauma bore down on believers with power to crush those who were fingered by their neighbors for the abrupt

---

46. On the function of extended metaphors, see Seland, "πάροικος," 247, who characterizes this text as a structural metaphor in which one concept is metaphorically structured in terms of another. See also Black, *Models and Metaphors*, 25–47.

47. See also Isa 49:23.

48. Hos 4:5; 5:5; 14:1; Mal 2:8; Isa 59:14; Jer 13:16; 20;10.

change in behavior they exhibited because of their new birth: "You have already spent enough time in doing what the Gentiles like to do.... They are surprised that you no longer join them in the same excesses of dissipation, and so they malign you" (4:3–4).

In crafting an epistle of consolation, the writer took on directly the reality of shame and what shame unanswered could do to wreck both trust in God's credibility and one's confidence in the limits of their ability not to collapse. The author insists that Jesus is the irreplaceable example of the one who cast himself utterly upon God within the abyss of the deepest shame of the cross and was vindicated by God.[49] The letter asserts in 4:16: Though you may be reviled and maligned for your hope in God, by casting yourself upon Jesus, God will not put you to shame, God will not abandon you.[50]

The key phrase "will not be put to shame" (οὐ μὴ καταισχυνθῇ) is quoted directly from LXX of Isa 28:16. This citation, managed through the technique of "association," which was described earlier in this chapter, gives the reader of the epistle access to the rich deposit of comfort in Isaiah.[51] Moreover, not only does the technique of association link the reader to additional texts in Isaiah, but the quotation is designed to "awaken," or trigger into the consciousness of the reader, additional underlying texts which expand the message of not being put to shame.[52]

While caution is necessary in identifying such texts, might the reader have "heard," for example, Ps 22:5 (LXX 21:5) "[our fathers] hoped in thee and were not ashamed (καὶ οὐ κατῃσχύνθησαν)"? As verse 6 shows, the one who is ashamed speaks of being a "worm." Psalm 25:2 (LXX 24:2) voices the plea, "O my God, I have trusted in thee; let me not be [put to shame] (μὴ καταισχυνθείην)" which is explained by the following cola "neither let my

---

49. Horrell, "The Label Χριστιανός," 380. "Jesus' death as a criminal on a cross marked him as a rebel who ended his days in degradation and shame, but the early Christians insisted that his death was instead a moment of glory and not shame, or, at least, this the verdict of the cross was reversed by the vindication of the resurrection."

50 Compare also 3:15–16, "Always be ready to make your defense to anyone who demands from you an accounting for the hope that is in you; yet do it with gentleness and reverence. Keep your conscience clear, so that, when you are maligned, those who abuse you for your good conduct in Christ may be put to shame." In the midst of your shame ("when you are maligned") you will be given new agency by which to respond in unexpected ways ("with gentleness and reverence") because of the "hope that is within you."

51 42:17; 49:9,11; 45:16,17; 49:23; 50:7; 54:4; 65:13.

52. See Thompson's analysis of the dynamics of allusion which "involves (1) the use of a sign or marker [within a given text] (2) that calls to the reader's mind another known text (3) for a specific purpose." *Clothed with Christ*, 29.

enemies laugh me to scorn." The speaker completes her confession by stating "For none of them that wait on thee shall in any wise be ashamed (καὶ γὰρ πάντες οἱ ὑπομένοντές σε οὐ μὴ καταισχυνθῶσιν)." These two examples describe the tight relationship between trust/waiting on God and not being put to shame. Breaking trust is being put to shame. Through such a process of association, the opportunity is created to bring other texts into play which intensify the claim that God will remain faithful to those who cast themselves on Jesus. Moreover, the emotive states of the psalm speakers who are struggling against subjugation and psychological assault resonate with the reviling and maligning of Peter's addressees.[53]

This study has identified a high concentration of allusions and citations drawn from Jonah, Hosea, Zephaniah, Malachi which frame this text from Isaiah. This prompts a search in the Twelve for additional texts with the potential of being "awakened" by the claim of not being put to shame. Such a text occurs in Joel 2:26–27, "And my people shall never again be put to shame" (καὶ οὐ μὴ καταισχυνθῇ ὁ λαός μου εἰς τὸν αἰῶνα), stated twice to underscore the result of God's restoration of God's people. The following analysis will suggest how this underlying text might add depth not only to the claim of 1 Pet 2:6 but also throw light on the allusion to Zech 13:9 in Peter's reference to "fiery trials."

The perfect match of vocabulary between Isa 28:16 and Joel 2:26–27 is consistent with a pattern practiced in Joel of aggregating several writings across the Twelve.[54] As Seitz has insightfully observed, Joel is "a prophet brokering older prophecy for a new day."[55] Clearly Joel shows the character-

53. See Watts, "Psalmody in Prophecy," 216.

54. What follows in this section summarizes and sometimes reproduces discussion in Bailey, *Living in the Language of God*, 42–51. See also Coggins, "Interbiblical Quotations in Joel," 77–84

55. Seizt, *Joel*, 10. For example, the visions in Amos of locusts, fire, fruit-become-judgment, darkness, and the LORD at the altar in judgment (7:1—9:4) reappear in Joel 1 and 2. Joel 3:16, 18 contains citations of Amos 1:2 and 9:13, respectively. Nogalski, "Reading the Book of the Twelve Theologically," 117, suggests that these citations, occurring at the beginning and end of Amos, indicate that Joel reaches out to encompass the Amos corpus. Seizt, *Joel*, 9, 60, comments that it is likely that "Joel's depiction of the character of God may well be forged in a conversation with the Book of Jonah (the King of Nineveh there speaks like Joel's hoped-for penitential addressants; compare Joel 2:12–14 and Jonah 3:9"; and "The ecological effects of God's judgment is a major theme of Hosea ('grain, wine and oil' of 2:8 and similar refrains in 2:9, 2:12, 2:22, 5:12, 8:7, 9:2,4, 9:14,16, 14:7), and it is reproduced in its own form in Joel." Joel 3:19 shows knowledge of Obad 8–14. The call to repentance in Joel 2:12–17 repeats major notes of Zeph 2:1–3. The placement of this call within the midst of the description of the terrible Day of the LORD

istics of a late composition. He learned from earlier prophets and modified what they said in his own presentation. Seitz explains, "Joel reaches out for the audience as inherent to its first and final purpose, and it does this through its brilliant modification of earlier prophetic discourse, suitable for its time and for its location and purpose within the Book of the Twelve."[56] From across the Twelve and beyond Joel selects texts and modifies them to support an important theological position.

The impact of Joel's promise that God's people will not be put to shame is appreciated by taking in the sweep of his entire prophecy. Seitz observes that the Day of the LORD, which we referenced in section 2 of this chapter, begins in Joel 1 as a natural disaster, a plague of locusts, that in time expands into a national disaster of an enemy overrun. In the midst of this evolving catastrophe, a call goes out to Israel in Joel 2:13–14 to engage in a ritual of repentance and appeal to God for salvation. This call is rooted in God's self-disclosure as a God of mercy (the self-designation formula which we outlined in chapter 1).

> Return to the LORD, your God,
> for he is gracious and merciful,
> slow to anger, and abounding in steadfast love,
> and relents from punishing.
> Who knows whether he will not turn and relent,
> and leave a blessing behind him,
> a grain offering and a drink offering
> for the LORD, your God?[57]

---

follows the pattern of Zech 13:7–9, where covenantal dialogue is promised in the midst of a massive refining "On that day."

56 Seitz, *Joel*, 47. Bulkeley, "The Book of Amos as 'Prophetic Fiction,'" 212–13 contributes a similar understanding: "Such a work [of prophetic fiction] presents prophetic figures and their preaching, with a possible but not a necessary connection to any historic prophets who may be identified. . . . I intend the word 'fiction,' not to imply the opposite of 'factual,' but . . . to underline the creativity of the writers, and to detach investigation of their works from an overriding concern for the historicity of the events (including speeches) they recount."

57. A close comparison of how Joel treats the foundational text of Exod 34:6–7, which we first encountered in our treatment of Jonah earlier in this chapter, reveals that the references to God "by no means clearing the guilty, but visiting the iniquity of the parents upon the children and the children's children, to the third and the fourth generation" are absent in the text (Joel 2:13) with reference to Israel and are replaced with "he relents from sending calamity." However, the substance of Exod 34:7 is the basis of the

Seitz expands on this point by noting that the "Who knows?" language of 2:14 "does not represent . . . 'nobody knows for sure.'"[58] Instead, it is a strong confession that YHWH's character, at its very essence, is such that room is always left for God's freedom to act in mercy. It is the prophet's sharp 'No' to the verdict [of judgment] being already final. The priestly intercession to follow is indeed efficacious. YHWH has pity on his people . . . . God is himself inside his own Day, the compassionate and merciful YHWH."[59] Therefore to the awesome question of 2:11 "Truly the day of the LORD is great; terrible indeed—who can endure it?" the answer is: Israel can for all time[60] (twice "my people shall never again be put to shame"). As the Day of the LORD marches to a crescendo throughout Joel 3 and 4, Israel is to be buoyed by the trust that God is in the midst of the terrible day with intent to save God's people.

This overview shows that Joel may be brought to bear to defend the claim of 1 Pet 2:6 ("the one who believes/trusts in him will not be put to shame"). In the unique situation within the struggle of those called to be faithful under testing, God is heavily invested in proving this claim. This yields a crucial aspect to 1 Peter's message of consolation. The trust of Jesus, the keystone, in God is tested in the shame of his crucifixion and validated in the resurrection, and the integrity of the spiritual temple, the stamina of the "living stones," under shaming is secured by cleaving to Jesus, the keystone.

As the following examples show, there is a tight interplay between the trust of Jesus in God, validated by resurrection, and the believer's cleaving. This interplay of defends against being put to shame when the testing occasions feeling God's abandonment.

1 Peter 1:18–21

> You know that you were ransomed from the futile ways inherited from your ancestors, not with perishable things like silver or gold, but with the precious blood of Christ, like that of a lamb without

---

concluding verse of Joel 4:21 (Eng 3:21) describing the judgment of the nations.

58. Seitz, *Joel*, 74. This quotation comes from Jeremias, "The Function of the Book of Joel," 82.

59. Seitz, *Joel* 75. See also a similar conclusion reached by Moberly, "God Is Not a Human," 114, "In a context whose imagery strongly emphasized absolute divine power, we have as strong a statement as possible of divine responsiveness to human attitude and action. *Where God is most free to act, God is most bound in that acting.*"

60 Seitz, *Joel*, 54.

1 Peter 2:21–23

For to this you have been called, because Christ also suffered for you, leaving you an example, so that you should follow in his steps.

"He committed no sin,
and no deceit was found in his mouth."

When he was abused, he did not return abuse; when he suffered, he did not threaten; but he entrusted himself to the one who judges justly.

1 Peter 3:14–15

But even if you do suffer for doing what is right, you are blessed. Do not fear what they fear, and do not be intimidated, but in your hearts sanctify Christ as Lord.

This interplay between God's faithfulness undergirding believer's stamina also shapes pithy, tightly composed phrases of encouragement such as "To you then who believe, he is [your] honor" (2:7); "Therefore, let those suffering in accordance with God's will entrust themselves to a faithful Creator, while continuing to do good" (4:19); "Cast all your anxiety on him, because he cares for you" (5:7); and "Resist him, steadfast (στερεοί) in your faith.... And after you have suffered for a little while, the God of all grace ... will himself restore, support (στηρίζει), strengthen, and establish you" (5:9–11).

5. Fiery Trials, 1 Peter 4:12

The "awakened" presence of Joel contributes to 1 Peter's use of Zechariah's image of fiery trials in 4:12.[61]

> Beloved, do not be surprised at the fiery ordeal that is taking place among you to test you, as though something strange were happening to you.

Zechariah 13:8–9 is generally considered to be the underlying reference text.

---

61 The image of being tested by fire was first used in 1:7.

> In the whole land, says the LORD,
> two-thirds shall be cut off and perish,
> and one-third shall be left alive.
> And I will put this third into the fire,
> refine them as one refines silver,
> and test them as gold is tested.
> They will call on my name,
> and I will answer them.
> I will say, "They are my people";
> and they will say, "The LORD is our God."

A brief summary of our discussion will prove helpful in considering the notion of fiery trials. In chapter 1 we considered Leibengood's use of this text as pointing to an underlying elaborate plan used by the author of 1 Peter, drawn from Zech 9–14, to explain why Christians must undergo fiery trials after Christ has been raised. While that question is urgent, our investigation did not support Leibengood's contention that this question drove the writing of 1 Peter. We were not convinced that the message of the epistle was an offer of a plan as the way to satisfy the crisis of remaining loyal under trial.

That evaluation, however, prompted us to continue to look for the purpose of the epistle which helps believers cope with the vagaries of socio-political realities of state-sponsored persecution. This search led to the insight recently offered by Holloway that 1 Peter is an epistle of consolation. Holloway argues that the letter consoles Christians by giving them a new identity counter to that of their former lives. They may deal with fiery trails by seeing themselves as people who are called out of this world into God's apocalyptic family and future.

While Holloway's placement of his addresses in an apocalyptic, world-denying family is questioned by many scholars, we believe Holloway has open up a fruitful line of inquiry by interpreting 1 Peter within the genre of consolation literature. This identification called our attention to its overlap with another book of consolation, The Book of the Twelve, so identified by Sirach.

The need for Christians to cope with fiery trials is not met as Holloway suggests through disidentifying with this world. The need is satisfied by maintaining one's hold on the faithfulness of God in the face of the terror of the fiery trial. So the question driving the writing of the epistle is: Will the faithfulness of God prove reliable in the face of the terror of the fiery trial? We will demonstrate how the author of 1 Peter drew from Zechariah in composing his letter of consolation to answer this question.

Zechariah 13:8–9 is situated between a chaotic series of events bringing judgment for foreign nations and restoration for Israel (Zech 9–10, 12). False shepherds and prophets are exposed and excoriated (Zech 11; 13:6) which leads to a general purging of two thirds of Israel, climaxed by the refining by fire of the final third (Zech 13:7–9). Judgment and restoration resume in Zech 14 with events of increasing shock and awe. Within this large block of text, Zech 13:7–9 scans as a poetic insertion into this overall scheme. The purge by fire results in a population who speaks the language of the covenant: "They will call on my name, and I will answer them. I will say, 'They are my people,' and they will say, 'The LORD is our God'" (v. 9).[62] The covenantal dialogue embedded in this poetic insertion is an instance of the blending of two statements of divine self-designation—"I will take you as my people, and I will be your God" (Exod 6:7) and "I will make all my goodness pass before you, and will proclaim before you the name, 'The LORD'" (Exod 33:18)—within the imagery of the terrors of the Day of the LORD.

It is noteworthy that there is nothing peculiar to this final third of the population which makes it able to withstand the fiery test and say the words of covenant loyalty. God simply takes responsibility for the positive outcome of this test by specifying what God's people will say and making it so. The positioning of this poetic section within a text of intensifying shock and awe inserts the claim that in the midst of the fire, God's people will find themselves enabled to remain true to their confession. They do not need to be surprised and disoriented—not because it is "predicted" or even because they have already prepared themselves mentally and spiritually for misfortune whenever it comes. Rather, they retrain their equipoise because they are prepared to be steadied by God's prior word of faithfulness. This is another instance of comfort and encouragement erupting in the midst of terror, first encountered in Joel 2:12–19 underlying 1 Pet 2:6 (Isa 48:16), which has the intention of undergirding stamina.

---

62 At a deep level the interpretation effects a looping back to 1 Pet 2:9–10 with the proclamation of the mighty acts, "Once . . . now; once . . . now."

Conclusion

Through a skillful employment of recognized exegetical practices, the author of 1 Peter shows knowledge of the canonical status of the Twelve as a book of consolation in at least five important instances in the writing of the epistle of comfort and encouragement. Because of overlapping interpretative grids, the author credits the Spirit with taking up what is received in Israel's scripture and vivifying this tradition to make it serve a new context, time, and community. The community of Christ-followers which functions as the steward of the grid is both a continuance with the community of Israel as well as a rupture. This sets up a certain level of tension between old and new.[63] We will address this tension in the next chapter as we consider the influence of the Twelve on 1 Peter in the widest context.

---

63 See Bauman-Martin, "Speaking Jewish: Postcolonial Aliens and Strangers in First Peter."

3

The Influence of the Twelve on Counter-Intuitive Identity in 1 Peter

Summary of the Investigation

AS WE HAVE PROGRESSED in our reading of 1 Peter, we have engaged its characterization of the addressees as sojourners and exiles repeatedly. Our position, along with many who have studied this letter, holds that this designation is new for these addressees, one that has been placed on them as a result of their being called by God to a new orientation. Thus, the label is metaphorical, not factual, and draws on standard ways of expressing religious conversion such as are found in Jewish proselytism. They have been reborn. Their new birth has resulted in a break with their former social groupings, customs, and loyalties, which has been caused by their joining with a new group, called Christian, with its unique ethic and belief. They have renounced fundamental aspects of their native identity for a new identity that, to the dominant culture, appears strange and alien. The consequence of this break puts them in jeopardy of being subjected to fiery trials when they are brought before a Roman tribunal and sets up the challenge of their remaining firm in their new identity.[1]

Recent scholarly interpretation of 1 Peter has been steadily coalescing around the notion that the letter puts forward a construction of Christian

---

1. Horrell's observation is exemplary: "This does not deny that the terms, at least in 1 Peter, are used to depict a sense of social alienation, or estrangement from the world due to the hostility of the wider society. It does however strongly suggest that the terms as used in 1 Peter do not reflect their use as socio-political designations in Graeco-Roman society but rather their use in Jewish tradition to express the alienation and estrangement of God's people from the world. The terms describe not the addresses' socio-legal status *prior* to conversion, but their socio-spiritual status *consequent* on their conversion." "Aliens and Strangers." 116. See also Green, "Faithful Witness in the Diaspora," 285, 288.

identity that runs counter to that which is expressed in the wider social world of the Roman Empire. Fundamentally, the constellation of terms that the letter uses to describe these Christians and the claims made about Jesus Christ displaces the salvific claims of the emperor and the claims of the empire as salvation.² The letter constructs this counter-identity with the express intent to offer encouragement to Christians who are bearing up under intense pressure to recant. The letter insists that adhering to this counter-identity is the only way to persevere against the pressure to recant and conform.

An important piece of this perseverance is the ability to offer an alternative way of responding to adversity. No longer are retaliation or servile submission the only options. Because of the believer's new counter-intuitive identity, the ability to bless one's opponents and to maintain self-respect in suffering are now available as strategies of response. Consequently, a witness can be made of the new world into which one has been born and an invitation be given to one's oppressors to be reborn.

This counter-identity is bound up in the name Christian, a word originally coined as a label of derision and criminality.³ In the hands of outsiders, the label became "the crucial identifier that determines whether a person is or is not a social deviant, whether they can be permitted to remain in society or not."⁴ The new identity label, focused as it is on Christ, drives the wearer of it to the life of Jesus who trusted God through the fiery trial of his crucifixion and experienced that trust validated through God raising him from the dead.

We have noted that the message of the resurrection of the crucified Christ offers three strategies for those under trial. First, the message creates a new hope in those who cling to him, for he is proof of an existence that is not subject to earth-bound power and possibility. Second, to those who are suffering shame and possible martyrdom, the message of the crucified Christ opens up a way for them to bond to him such that by virtue of that

---

2. Horrell, "Between Conformity," 132.

3. Horrell, "Between Conformity," 141." *Christianoi* is a Latinism, a label created by hostile outsiders, probably Roman which . . . represents a negative judgment of this group." The Christian's self-disassociations from established patterns of politico-religious practice—the refusal to play their part in sustaining the *pax decorum* on which the *pax romana* depended—could well have made them unpopular and led to their being viewed as antisocial criminals [such as murderers and thieves] who hated the rest of the human race," 140. See also Seland, "πάροικος," 264, "In a society so saturated with the values of honor and shame, these slanders, revilings, and abuses were great obstacles to social integration in local communities."

4. Horrell, "The Label Χριστιανός," 376.

bond in suffering they have access a new hope for perseverance in their being tested based upon cleaving to the suffering one who was raised from the dead.[5] Third, to all who struggle to live faithfully as aliens and sojourners in a hostile dominant culture, the behavior of the crucified Christ offers an alternative way of responding to threat. This alternative preserves the agency of the threatened one and exemplifies a new way of living which is on offer to the dominant power to adopt. Through this complex strategy, the one whose honor is stripped publicly is given Christ's honor.

Such a way of thinking is counter-factual, counter-intuitive. It begins out of a state of disorientation and dislocation and leads to reorienting and relocating which is abundantly clear from the start of the letter: "Although you have not seen him, you love him; and even though you do not see him now, you believe in him and rejoice with an indescribable and glorious joy, for you are receiving the outcome of your faith, the salvation of your souls" (1 Pet 1:8–9).

This counter-factual way of regarding oneself is the irreducible ingredient of the comfort of the letter. Of course, this prominent feature is not unique to this letter. It is shared with the entire sweep of the Bible's witness. Within this broader context, our investigation is narrowly focused on how the counter-factual thinking of 1 Peter resonates with the Twelve, making all the clearer the indebtedness of the epistle to this section of the Hebrew Bible. As we focus closely on how the Twelve could have guided the formation of one's identity as a Christian in hostile circumstances, it will be helpful to be reminded of the overriding intention of the Twelve.

Recalling our previous discussion, the Book of the Twelve is constructed out of the writings of twelve prophets to confront and address in various ways the double-headed challenge (1) are God's people capable of being faithful to God in the light of overwhelming evidence of willful and persistent disobedience, and (2) can God be trusted to follow through on God's promise to be faithful when that credibility is threatened by evidence of God's impotency. The existential crisis which these challenges provoke can be measured by the questions evoked in two books which frame the collection: "Truly the day of the LORD is great; terrible

---

5. Feldmeier, *The First Letter of Peter*, 94, points out that the unusual plural of suffering in 1:11 indicates the intention of the author to open the application of the cross to the oppression of the persecuted believers.

indeed—who can endure it?" (Joel 2:11, repeated in Mal 3:2) and "Where is the God of justice?" (Mal 2:17).[6]

To be sure, the Twelve is aimed at the necessities of remaining faithful in the post-exilic era. However, these questions remain central to the ongoing life of God's people. Our investigation of 1 Peter shows how these questions re-emerge as the dominating issues of the community of exiles and sojourners in Asia Minor. The letter asserts that Jesus is the exemplar of engaging the challenge of faithfulness under threat. He entrusted himself to God's faithfulness even through death on a cross, and God proved God's faithfulness to him by raising him from the dead. The two questions which dominate the Twelve, human capability and divine credibility, coalesce in the one man. The evangelical call is: The one who believes/trusts in him will not be put to shame. It is finally what happens to Jesus that establishes the counter-factual identity of his followers.

While textual linkage is sparse, three nodes in the Twelve come to the forefront as potential influences on the author of 1 Peter in forming counter-factual identity.

1. Habakkuk 3:17–19

In studying the Twelve, the writer of 1 Peter would have encountered a striking example of a statement of counter-factual identity in Hab 3:17–19. The baseline against which this statement is lodged begins in Hab 1 with two laments (vv. 2–4, 12–17) in liturgical style which express the shame of experiencing God's impassivity in the face of foreign domination. This threat to divine capability is processed through Hab 2 whose conclusion "The LORD is in his holy temple; let all the earth be silent before him" prepares the reader for the theophany of the Day of the LORD described in an inset hymn in Hab 3:13.[7]

> You came out to deliver your people,
> to save your anointed one.
> You crushed the leader of the land of wickedness,
> you stripped him from head to foot.

---

6. See Bailey, *Living in the Language of God*, 9.
7. On inset hymns, see Watts, "Psalmody in Prophecy," 211.

What is striking is that the vision of salvation which has been sung is not yet realized as 3:16 makes clear;

> I hear, and I tremble within;
> my lips quiver at the sound.
> Rottenness enters into my bones,
> and my steps tremble beneath me.
> I wait quietly for the day of calamity
> to come upon the people who attack us.

Watts has observed, "the tension between oppressive reality (chs. 1–2) and salvific hope (3:2–15) remains taut to the end." In this situation of indeterminacy, Hab 3:17–18 records a counter-intuitive position:

> Though the fig tree does not bud
> and there are no grapes on the vines,
> though the olive crop fails
> and the fields produce no food,
> though there are no sheep in the pen
> and no cattle in the stalls,
> yet I will rejoice in the Lord,
> I will be joyful in God my Savior.

Though the poetic sweep of this statement of joy in the midst of nothingness is astonishing, what is stunning is that its language is a bridge between the utter collapse of the human frame previously described in 3:16 and the following v. 19, which brings to a strong climax this book:

> God, the Lord, is my strength;
> he makes my feet like the feet of a deer,
> and makes me tread upon the heights.

Here we encounter the demonstration that casting oneself utterly on God ("I will wait quietly") opens access to this counter-factual stance which yields its blessings of rejoicing and new agency.

While no textual connection can be forged between Hab 1–3 and 1 Peter, we suggest that the poetic reflection of the struggle between fact and counter-fact resonates deeply with the statement of first principles in 1 Pet 1:8–9: "Though you have not seen him, you love him; and even though you do not see him now, you believe in him and are filled with an inexpressible and glorious joy, for you are receiving the end result of your faith, the salvation of your souls." This foundational statement works in tandem with the plan of the epistle's author to insert his addressees "into a (Jewish) narrative of identity that *dislocates* them from the empire and invites them into a self-understanding based on the experience of dispersion and alienation."[8] To say with certainty that Habakkuk was in the mind of the epistle's author would be unjustified, but it is not hard to imagine its influencing the argument of the epistle at a fundamental level.

2. Micah 7:1–10

In summary form, Mic 7 describes a situation *in extremis* where the speaker is surrounded by a total absence of faithful and upright people (vv. 1–4a, 5–7). The prophet presents a panorama of deception reaching down into the most intimate of relationships. In the midst of this desert of hostility, a new day is announced bringing total confusion to this population (v. 4b).[9] This announcement of God's intervention brings forth a confession from the speaker of total trust in God and God's salvation (v. 7). In spite of all that is thrown against the one threatened, the speaker's confession persists: "But as for me, I will look to the LORD, I will wait for the God of my salvation; my God will hear me."

Then follows a speech to the enemies where the speaker lays bare the assumptions on which the speaker's confidence is based (vv. 8–9). The enemies are commanded not to rejoice over their domination because such rejoicing brings on the day of God's judgment and salvation. As the enemy rejoices in the embedded speech "Where is the LORD your God?" (v. 10), it triggers its downfall as God answers that question with Israel's vindication, light, and salvation. The onset of confusion and shame is God's response to hostile, haughty speech.

Central to what the vulnerable say to the enemies is a confession of counter-intuitive identity. Micah 7:8–10 warns the oppressor not to read off victory from the collapse of the vulnerable: "Do not rejoice over me, O my enemy; when I fall, I shall rise; when I sit in darkness the LORD will be a light to Me. . . . He will bring me out to the light; I shall see his vindication. Then

---

8. Horrell, "Aliens and Strangers," 131.

9. For a discussion of the setting of this chapter in the time of Sennacherib's siege of Jerusalem in 701, see Sweeney, *The Twelve Prophets*, II, 405–6.

my enemy will see, and shame will cover him who said to me, 'Where is the LORD your God?'" The enemies heap shame against the one whose vulnerable state is proof of the absence of God. However, this shame is ultimately turned against the enemy, and the vulnerable are shown to possess an identity which is bound up in trust that survives beyond their collapse.

While 1 Peter makes no direct textual tie to Mic 7, the chapter presents attractive opportunities for the community reading the epistle to resonate with the prophet's struggles, and in the community's use of it be formed to act counter-intuitively. One can imagine that Mic 7:5–6: "Put no trust in a friend, have no confidence in a loved one, guard the doors of your mouth from [the one] who lies in your embrace; for . . . your enemies are members of your own household" would strike a responsive chord in the hearing of wives of unbelieving husbands or slaves of unbelieving masters. Within this hearing, wives and slaves can take up the prophet's strong words of assurance of vindication.

Against all odds, the epistle makes the counter-claim that by entrusting one's life to Jesus, persons whose societal vulnerability has been made worse by their faith can respond non-defensively to their oppressors with the hope of liberating their oppressors from their own fears.[10] Some of the letter's most pointed encouragement is directed to those made most vulnerable:

To slaves: "If you endure when you do right and suffer for it, you have God's approval . . . . When [Christ] was abused, he did not return abuse; when he suffered, he did not threaten; but he entrusted himself to the one who judges justly" (1 Pet 2:20b, 23).

To wives: "Wives, in the same way, accept the authority of your husbands, so that even if some of them do not obey the word, they may be won over without a word by their wives' conduct . . . as long as you do what is good and never let fears alarm you" (1 Pet 3:1, 6).

This specific encouragement is grounded in the recognition of living under harsh realities of limited options, and the compromises and trade-offs that may be required—all of which are bracketed and qualified by utter trust in the ultimate justice of God.

However, it was not only those made most vulnerable who were threatened. The epistle addresses a general audience of believers who are

---

10 Feldmeier, "1 Peter The 'Nation' of Strangers," 259 comments: "the significance given the situation from a theological perspective enables it to be accepted and so releases energies tied up by resistance."

made liable to exposure and prosecution by the guardians of the religion of the state. Similarly, Mic 7:2–3 describes the faithful being netted by those who "lie in wait for blood" and brought before a hostile and corrupt justice system. This is language which would speak to those in 1 Peter's audience who had been exposed to Roman prosecutorial powers and forthwith shamed and physically hurt.

To this general audience the epistle counsels: "Conduct yourselves honorably among the Gentiles, so that though they malign you as evildoers, they may see your honorable deeds and glorify God when he comes to judge.... Fear God. Honor the emperor" (1 Pet 2:12, 17b) and "Do not fear what they fear, and do not be intimidated, but in your hearts sanctify Christ as Lord. Always be ready to make your defense to anyone who demands from you an accounting for the hope that is in you, yet do it with gentleness and reverence" (1 Pet 3. 14b–16a).

The intent of these words of counsel is to protect threatened persons from being swamped by fear by giving them new agency such that their behavior has promise of redeeming the very structures of oppression. Thus, vindication comes in the form of the new birth of the enemy! In this light, the vision of 1 Peter goes beyond the stated expectations of Micah who sees vindication solely in terms of an enemy's downfall.[11] The foundation underlying 1 Peter's audacious claim to redeem someone hostile is the faithfulness God proves in the resurrection of the crucified Christ to whom the believer must be entrusted.

3. Malachi 3:13–18

In chapter 2 we considered this text more narrowly as the source for calling the epistle's readers "God's own people" (2:9). A fuller appreciation of Malachi shows how its enunciating a counter-factual position contributes in a major way to the comfort of God's people under severe stress.

In the closing verses of Malachi, the community is coping with an impending collapse of its stamina to remain faithful to God. This crisis is set up by God's promise to bless and make happy those who are faithful with their tithes and worship. The faithful challenge God's integrity in

---

11. However, 1 Pet 3:16, "Keep your conscience clear, so that, when you are maligned, those who abuse you for your good conduct in Christ may be put to shame" states a traditional motif of apocalyptic expectation. Yet 4:4–6 and perhaps 3:19–20 may suggest the Rejected One makes common cause with those rejecting to lead them to salvation.

the light of God's justice being put to shame by arrogant people whose prosperity and happiness incite their impunity toward God (Mal 3:15). A crisis of faith in God is resolved when "those who revered the Lord spoke with one another." The Lord took note and listened, and a "book of remembrance was written before him of those who revered the Lord and thought on his name" (Mal 3:16). Those who revered the Lord used words to think "on his name." While the intriguing phrase, "those who thought on his name" has no parallel in the Old Testament, a similar phrase, "When I think of your ways, I turn my feet to your testimonies," is found in Ps 119:59, a suggestive description of confessional thinking leading to confessionally shaped behavior.

Malachi's community which survives the buffeting of doubt can be put into sharper focus by analyzing the book of remembrance which was written before the Lord of/for those who revered the Lord and thought on his name. Nogalski has made the constructive observation that the book of remembrance was not a record of the faithful speakers, not a book of life, but a record of faithful speaking, written *for* Godfearers to be consulted by future generations of those who revered and spoke of God's name.[12] He argues that the book of remembrance (ספר זכרון) has a parallel citation in Exod 17:14 "a reminder in a book" (בספר זכרון) which Moses is commanded to read in the hearing of Joshua. Also, he cites Esth 6:1 as a close parallel where "the book of records, the annals ... were read to the king" when he could not sleep. Furthermore, Nogalski shows that לפניו ליראי יהוה "of/for those who revered the Lord" (Mal 3:16) has a parallel in Josh 8:32 referencing the copy of the law of Moses which he "wrote in the presence of the Israelites" (כתב לפני). Thus the community is marked by an awareness of the sacral or liturgical dimension of speaking (before the Lord) with a clear eye toward scribal activity to preserve such speech.[13] The record thus created serves as a guide for future generations to be faithful, that is, to be able to discern (again!) the difference between the righteous and the wicked.

Malachi opens up the intriguing aspect of a liturgical setting in which to nurture counter-intuitive positioning. Malachi's community finds itself mirrored in Ps 73, where one who is weary of finding any reason to trust in

---

12. Nogalski, "How Does Malachi's 'Book of Remembrance,'" 191–96.

13. Nogalski, *Two Sides of a Coin*, 33, draws attention to the cultic materials in the Twelve and suggests locating the final shaping of the Twelve in the Persian period world of Judah. See also, 40–46.

God is driven into the sanctuary wherein an insight is given which confirms persevering in trust in God's integrity. This results in the counter-intuitive assertion, "My flesh and my heart may fail, but God is the strength of my heart and my portion forever" (v. 26).[14] Malachi's speakers "have their counterpart in him 'who is humble and contrite in spirit, and trembles at my word'" (Isa 66:2).[15] Worship is the place where God strengthens faithfulness through the frank exchanges of pain and disappointment combined with reaching out in confession and the embrace of divine mercy. The lamenters of Malachi are held within the liturgical power of the name of God and the givenness of the text.[16]

Even if the writer of 1 Peter was not conscious of the model in Malachi, the importance of worship to the epistle's author for the flourishing of counter-intuitive identity clearly patterned after that of the prophet. Being counter-factual, this identity does not grow from ideas which are biologically given, whose meaning is dictated by nature. We have already noted how Christian identity is a social construction. Social constructions of identity are ultimately constructed through written and spoken discourse and as such identity has to be maintained by reiterated practices and discursive strategies.[17] This identity grows, layer by layer, through communal liturgies surrounding belief and confession. This is, operationally speaking, the substance of worship.[18]

The role of ritual behavior has often been discounted as a pathological escape into cult by powerless people. Recent thinking, however, leads to the important suggestion that "ritual is a means of protecting social boundaries, and thus a creative mechanism."[19] Indeed, 1 Pet 1:15–16 encourages, "Be holy as I [God] am holy."[20]

---

14. Bailey, *The Self-Shaming God*, 47–48.

15. Seitz, "What Lesson Will History Teach?" 462

16. See the suggestive essays by Robinson, *The Givenness of Things*.

17 Horrell, "'Race', 'Nation', 'People,'" 158, quoting from Hall, *Ethnic Identity*, 2, 41 and Brett, "Interpreting Ethnicity," 10. See also Bailey, *Living in the Language of God*, 127–28.

18. For a useful introduction to the identity-forming power of worship see Wall, "With Voices United," 3–16.

19. Smith, *The Religion of the Landless*, 80–84, 203.

20. For an interpretation of the epistle which is structured on the issue of holiness, see Green, "Living as Exiles," which is discussed in chapter 5.

The epistle is laced with elements of worship. While an earlier theory the letter being structured as a baptismal sermon has fallen out of favor,[21] there are strong indications to support its intended use in worship. It is specifically addressed to a circle of churches in Anatolia with the purpose of being read as a letter of encouragement to Christian communities under fire. After the epistolary greeting (1:1–2), the letter begins with "Blessed" a liturgical word signaling a prayer.[22] Other doxologies and eulogies occur in 4:11, 5:11, 14b. Those who have been reborn by the word are to regard themselves as living stones built into Jesus, the keystone, becoming a spiritual temple wherein, as holy priests, they are to offer spiritual sacrifices acceptable to God (2:4–6). God's special people, sired by the word, are "to proclaim the mighty acts of him who called you out of darkness into his marvelous light" (2:9). The Psalms are quoted in 2:7 (Ps 118:22) and 3:10–12 (Ps 34:12–16). 1 Peter 5:8 contains an allusion to Ps 22:21.[23] As well, other hymnic fragments show up in 1:3, 18; 2:21; 3:18; 5:3.[24]

Both Malachi and 1 Peter assert that God will confirm the hard work of God's people who are engaged in an ongoing struggle to live faithfully in the midst of pressure to lapse into moral cynicism and theological despair. Malachi's community of speakers, like the circle of Anatolian churches, shape themselves around the gift of God's bifocal nature of graciousness and justice and use this gift to cultivate passionate theological talk which faces front-on the challenges at hand. This community is carried by the promise that their faithfulness will be upheld by the God who is both unstintingly merciful and maintains clear expectations.

Conclusions

Certainly the counter-intuitive behavior and affirmations of the Twelve resonate with the claims of the letter. Two consequences stem from the intriguing consideration that these textual blocks, in addition to the textual citations investigated in the preceding chapter, exercised the imagination of the epistle's author, informing the consolation he provides.

---

21. See Schutter, *Hermeneutic and Composition*, 82–83, for a summary of this discussion.
22. Holloway, *Coping with Prejudice*, 140–41.
23. Horrell, "Visuality, Vivid Description, and the Message of 1 Peter," 697–716.
24. Schutter, *Hermeneutic and Composition*, 35.

First, this robust use of the Hebrew Bible counters the point advanced by some that 1 Peter takes over Israel's scripture and empties it of its distinctive witness in a supersessionist interpretation.²⁵ For example, New Testament feminist scholar Elizabeth Schüssler Fiorenza criticizes Horrell because he

> seeks to have his cake and eat it at one and the same time when he claims that 1 Peter is positing postcolonial resistance to the Empire while at the same time advocating adaptation to imperial kyriarchal society. In the process, however, he empties the designation *Christianos* of all messianic connotations and solidifies a supersessionist reading of the text. In so doing he not only depoliticizes the rhetoric of the letter but also reads it over and against Judaism. It is the church who is now "the people of G*d." In the process, the presence and voices of the recipients have been lost. The voice of the author(s) has become absolute.²⁶

Horrell acknowledges the takeover of Israel's scriptures, but observes that the epistle is silent on the status of Israel itself. He shows how conversion requires being given a new history which Israel's scripture supplies.

> 1 Peter is simply silent about the continued existence of what Paul elsewhere called ὁ Ἰσραὴλ κατὰ σαρκά (1 Cor 10:18). There is no direct claim here that the church lays claim to an identity that is at the same time denied to Israel, no assertion that Israel's covenant is now obsolete or that Christians are now able to be and to enjoy all that Israel failed to attain. There is simply silence about such comparisons.²⁷

Furthermore, tracing how the epistle interacts with large blocks of Old Testament source material fixes the tension within the community on the issue of communal behavior rather than on communal status, a view helpfully advocated by Betchler. He focuses on how the letter speaks to the

---

25. See Bauman-Martin, "Speaking Jewish: Postcolonial Aliens and Strangers in First Peter." Liebengood's position clearly presupposes that the community that receives 1 Peter is of Jewish origin. He makes his argument for Jesus as eschatological Davidic Shepherd ("Confronting Roman Imperial Claims") exclusively on his program of 1 Peter's use of Zechariah. This would only be understandable to persons already steeped in the nuances of Hebrew Scripture. The flaws in his program are effectively pointed out by Foster, "Echoes without Resonance," as well as the general criticism of Bauman-Martin.

26. Fiorenza, *1 Peter*, 46. Fiorenza's position will be discussed in chapter 6.

27. Horrell, "'Race', 'Nation', 'People,'" 162.

status of the addressees' social liminality instead of behavior that stems from a counter-intuitive identity.

> They are neither fully integrated members of society nor entirely removed from it. They have made a clean break with the past and yet their obedience to God entails conduct in accordance with certain society conventions. For these readers who accept 1 Peter's constellation of metaphors as constitutive of their identity, social alienation is valorized as the will of God, as the corollary to their divine election, and as the authentic expression of the vocation to which God has called them as God's own people. Their social liminality, thus, need not be a threat to their personal integrity as long as they recognize that they are members of an alternative social entity and that this alternative community provides their plausibility structure over against the claims—and threats—of the larger society.[28]

We agree that liminality colors the epistle throughout. However, we argue that this liminality stems from the believer's identity lodged in the crucified-resurrected Christ. Divine election is for the purpose of valorizing Christ as Lord which issues in behavior (vocation) that has the potential to cause one to experience the fiery trial. The Christian's being neither "here" nor "there" is because their identity is in Christ, and it is from Christ that they receive an honor which persists through shame and remains unvanquished. From this vantage point they lay claim to Israel's history to call their own, for it, too, conveys a life upheld in the midst of shame and diaspora.[29] Their new history now describes their ability to seize new agency to confront their threats.

Nowhere is the letter's comfort of counter-intuitive identity more intense than in the paragraph that brings to a stunning conclusion its theological argument (4:12–16). We have already pointed out how the section begins with a standard formula of comfort, "Beloved, do not be surprised at the fiery ordeal that is taking place among you to test you, as though something strange were happening to you." What is surprising is the counter-factual response to this ordeal.

> But rejoice insofar as you are sharing Christ's sufferings, so that you may also be glad and shout for joy when his glory is revealed. If you are reviled for the name of Christ, you are blessed, because

---

28. Betchler, *Following in His Steps*, 155–56.
29. See Smith, *The Religion of the Landless*, 201–15.

the spirit of glory, which is the Spirit of God, is resting on you. But let none of you suffer as a murderer, a thief, a criminal, or even as a mischief maker. Yet if any of you suffers as a Christian, do not consider it a disgrace, but glorify God because you bear this name.

The author underscores the encouragement of the letter in three tightly compacted sentences describing counter-intuitive identity. Each of these sentences follows a pattern of facing reality, responding counter-factually and confessing utter reliance on God's faithfulness. The following table illustrates this pattern:

Reality	Counter-Factual	Rooted in Faithfulness
Fiery Ordeal.	Do not be surprised. Rejoice.	Participate in Christ's sufferings. Overjoyed at his appearing.
Reviled for the name of Christ.	You are blessed.	Spirit of glory/Spirit of God resting on you.
Suffer as a Christian as a murderer would suffer.	Do not consider it a disgrace, but praise God.	You bear his name.

With such stirring words the epistle reaches out in comfort to steady those who because of their being newly born into the sufferings and vindication of Christ must make their way as strangers in their own land.

4

The Use of 1 Peter by Aliens in the Modern Era, Part 1—Dietrich Bonhoeffer

IN THE PREVIOUS CHAPTERS, we have built the case for understanding 1 Peter as a letter written to Christians who attracted prosecutorial attention by their refusal to participate in political, religious, and other social activities they once enjoyed as non-Christians. The calumny they suffered extended from private abuse to localized public shaming, prosecution and punishment, including execution. They became aliens in their own country. The intention of this letter is to foster a counter-identity that can endure in the face of persecution, an identity that is centered on the crucified Christ's solidarity with them through shared suffering, which brings them into the hope of sharing in his validation by resurrection. The use the author made of the Book of the Twelve has contributed significantly to the development of this message.

Our study has proceeded on the position established by Horrell and others that the readers of 1 Peter are for the most part native-born who have become "alien" by virtue of their conversion to Christ as Lord. This is in distinction to a position previously articulated by Elliott in *A Home for the Homeless* that the aliens addressed are non-native populations who have been forcibly re-settled as part of imperial policy. Who the addressees are has Christological implications. For Elliott, Jesus functions as the figure around whom non-native populations can find a home in a sect. For Horrell, Jesus provides an identity into which the believer can be sealed which offers access to support in order to come through fiery trial.

It is time now to ask the question: how has 1 Peter been accessed in the modern era? The question can be framed from the methodological perspective: What evidence can be presented which shows how understandings of alien-ship influence interpretations of the letter? The question can also be structured from the pastoral viewpoint: Have modern readers who are made to feel aliens in their native land because of their confession of Christ as Lord also received insight and support from this first-century writing?

We will present our findings in this and the following chapter. We begin with an analysis of the use Dietrich Bonhoeffer (1906–45) made of 1 Peter. Of course, he predates the interpretation of the epistle with which we have been concerned up to now. Chapter 5 contains a discussion with scholars who have had the benefit of the path-breaking work of Horrell, Elliott, and Balch. While in the present chapter we will be examining material created long before the contemporary discussion of sociological alternatives, we need to remind ourselves that Bonhoeffer showed his ability for describing the sociological dimensions of the church-community in his book *Sanctorum Communio*.

In light of the extensive study of Bonhoeffer's life and thought, it will suffice to state that his work as a Lutheran pastor and theologian in the Confessing Church's resistance to German Christianity amply illustrates his struggle to live faithfully for Christ in his native land of Nazi Germany. He became as such as an alien in his native land. Bonhoeffer illustrates how important a Christological center is for native-born aliens in order to stay grounded as they grapple with their alien-ship in their own land. He anticipates to that degree Horrell's investigation of the situation of becoming Christian in 1 Peter.

During his struggle, Bonhoeffer played several roles: pastor, professor of theology to clandestine seminarians, conspirator in a plot to assassinate Adolf Hitler, prisoner of the Gestapo, and finally victim of hanging for treason.[1] Despite his relatively short life, he produced a prodigious body of writing: sermons, biblical studies, theological papers, plays, poetry, books, and letters. This body of work illustrates that Bonhoeffer wrote principally to strengthen the church's integrity and witness against a demonic state.

I argue that Bonhoeffer finds in 1 Peter an author whose pastoral and theological concerns resonated with his own. In the rest of this chapter I will trace how central 1 Peter is to the maturation of Bonhoeffer's theology and his personal, costly witness as a native-born alien.

Bonhoeffer's use of 1 Peter shows up as early as his years as pastor in Barcelona in 1928–29. His reading of the text at that time, of course, did

---

1. For a succinct overview of his life, see Barnett's introduction to Bonhoeffer, *"After Ten Years."* For a fuller accounting see Bethge's *Dietrich Bonhoeffer, A Biography*.

not have the looming Nazi threat in view. However, as early as May and July 1933, verses from 1 Pet 1 are cited which clearly have the threat of the Nazi takeover of the church on the horizon. Our analysis will proceed from this point forward. The period containing the most concentrated number of appeals to the letter is 1937–38, at the height of the resistance against the German Church, with eleven citations from 1 Pet 1, 2, 4, and 5. The years 1939–45 see fewer appearances, five total, but these are generative of some of Bonhoeffer's most searching thinking. In addition, our analysis will include two samples from his work which do not contain Petrine texts but whose content informs Bonhoeffer's link to 1 Peter.

In the aggregate, these numbers are impressive. 1 Peter is a letter of only five chapters. Bonhoeffer ranged throughout scripture to inform his work as pastor, professor, and conspirator. Yet as will become clear, he had a special affinity for 1 Peter. He heard the first-century letter to those who found themselves aliens in their native land speaking directly to his situation. He was further attracted to 1 Peter for its ability to describe complex issues threatening the life of the church within the framework of a classical Christology. He employed the normal channels of pastoral use of Bible: sermons, catechesis, meditations, and biblical studies.[2]

From this short overview, it is clear that our data will come from a span of twelve years in which rapid changes took place among German Christians. In order to analyze Bonhoeffer's use of 1 Peter over these years, a grid of five questions will be used. These questions are contained in his famous essay "After Ten Years." He wrote this piece at Christmas, 1942, and sent it to his brother-in-law Hans von Dohnanyi, to his close friend and colleague Eberhard Bethge, and to Major General Hans Oster, a German military officer in intelligence work who shared Bonhoeffer's views about the necessity to overthrow the Nazi regime.[3] Victoria Barnett introduces his reflections this way: "[T]he essay was a retrospective analysis of what had happened to them, and more broadly, what had happened to his church, his country, and his compatriots in the decade that had passed since the Nazis

---

2. Bonhoeffer's use of 1 Peter has escaped those who have studied his thought. Usually the only place where scholars cite his use of 1 Peter is in the story of his last brief meditation given to a small group of prisoners before his execution, 1 Pet 1:3, the content of which we do not have. See Nelson, "The Life of Dietrich Bonhoeffer," 44 and Godsey, *The Theology of Dietrich Bonhoeffer*, 202.

3. See her introduction to *"After Ten Years"* for extensive background to this essay. Barnett calls attention to the extermination of over 4 million Jews by December 1942, and numerous failed coups to remove Hitler from power.

came to power.... 'After Ten Years' was written, then, as a synthesis of an ongoing and troubled conversation between these men as they wrestled with their consciences and the diminishing options open to those who sought the end of National Socialism."[4]

These five programmatic questions in the essay represent broad themes on which Bonhoeffer worked throughout his short life. As this essay reflects on what he has learned and observed over the most important decade of his life, these questions assume a special urgency. Guided by them our analysis of his use of 1 Peter will achieve some cohesiveness. As we examine each item of his output in chronological order, we will be better able to mark the various ways he calls upon 1 Peter to advance his pastoral leadership.

The questions appear at the opening of the essay as if to structure what follows. While they are presented in the essay as a complete paragraph, they are listed here serially.[5]

1. Have there ever been people in history who in their time, like us, had so little ground under their feet, people to whom every possible alternative open to them at the time appeared equally unbearable, senseless, and contrary to life?

2. Have there been those who like us looked for the source of their strength beyond all those available alternatives? Were they looking entirely in what has passed away and in what is yet to come?

3. And, nevertheless, without being dreamers, did they await with calm and confidence the successful outcome of their endeavor?

4. Or rather, facing a great historical turning point, did the responsible thinkers of another generation ever feel differently than we do today—precisely because something genuinely new was forming that was not yet apparent in the existing alternatives?

5. Who Stands Firm?

The questions point to five themes which Bonhoeffer identifies as most important in structuring his efforts to serve the church in its present crisis.

1. Existence as an exile in one's native land with the concomitant challenges of living a compromised life.

---

4. Barnett, *"After Ten Years,"* 4.
5 Barnett, *"After Ten Years,"* 18.

2. Confessing the location of one's strength outside the bounds of what is humanly possible.

3. The new-found ability to deal with reality in a spirit of calm and confidence.

4. The new-found counter-intuitive identity centered on the cross of Christ.

5. The ability to endure.

Based on what we have presented as the core of 1 Peter, it is clear that Bonhoeffer's questions resonated with the text of the epistle. We will now describe how Bonhoeffer made use of the letter to develop his themes by examining nine extracts from the Bonhoeffer corpus. It will be helpful to remember that these nine writings are not meant as sequential illustrations of each of the five questions/themes. Rather, we will see how all five questions/themes taken together are developed by tracing in chronological order their varied appearance in these extracts.

1. Sermon on 1 Peter 1:7b–9, given in Berlin, Ascension Day, May 25, 1933

This sermon is preached within the context of the State's action in March 1933, abolishing all human rights and freedoms which entailed "freedom of speech, the press, public assembly, parliamentary controls, the privacy of post, telegraph and telephone; the identification of opposition to the government with hostility to the nation)."[6] Bonhoeffer's close friend and biographer, Eberhard Bethge, notes that almost nobody in the church publicly criticized this action. He explains, "Instead, churchmen applauded the establishment of order, the rescue of the nation from the liberalistic-democratic decay, protection against the threat of Bolshevism, the putting into effect of the Lutheran doctrine of the orders of creation, and the abolition of the consequences of the Versailles Treaty."[7] This was followed in April by the law "For the Reconstruction of the Civil Service" which placed Jews "on

---

6. Bethge, *Bonhoeffer: Exile and Martyr*, 69.

7. Bethge, *Bonhoeffer: Exile and Martyr*. While Bethge's works will be the primary historical source, see also the fine biographies of Marsh, *Strange Glory* and Schlingensiepen, *Dietrich Bonhoeffer 1906–1945*.

a separate legal basis on racial grounds, making them second-class citizens for purely biological reasons."[8]

Bonhoeffer had begun lecturing at the University of Berlin in 1932. His inaugural course was called "The Nature of the Church" which was followed in 1933 by a series on "Christology." Meanwhile, the Reich conference of German Christians held on April 3–4, 1933, "triggered radical changes at all levels of the church" under the heavy influence of Nazi officials. "The slogans of the conference were *Gleichschaltung* (the alignment of all sectors with Nazi goals), the *Führer* Principle, the Reich church, and racial conformity. . . . People of 'alien blood' . . . had no place in the pulpit and should not be allowed to be married before German Protestant altars."[9]

In contrast to widespread silence of the German Church over the attack on the Jews, Bonhoeffer delivered a paper "The Church and the Jewish Question" to a group of Berlin ministers in April 1933, in which he set out the theological grounds for the Church's struggle with National Socialism. He read this paper at a time when "hardly anybody in the Church was prepared to touch the subject," Bethge recalls. One member of the group objected to it, and another, Leonhard Fendt, the great Berlin preacher and professor of practical theology, left the meeting.[10]

While analyzing the content of this essay is not required, it is noteworthy that Bethge observes that this piece "marks a certain break in Bonhoeffer's life . . . . The problem of the authenticity of the Church in an increasingly threatening situation changed Bonhoeffer's way of speaking about the Church, made [his speaking] more critical of her privileges and grounded it afresh in Christology."[11]

This is the context in which Bonhoeffer was invited to preach on May 25, 1933, Ascension Day.[12] His text was 1 Pet 1:7b–9:

8. Bethge, *Bonhoeffer: Exile and Martyr*, 66.
9. Bethge, *Dietrich Bonhoeffer*, 170.
10. Bethge, *Bonhoeffer: Exile and Martyr*, 66 and 106.
11. Bethge, *Bonhoeffer: Exile and Martyr*, 69.
12. In the introduction of Lukens, Barnett, and Brocker to Bonhoeffer's sermons, collected in volume 11 of his collected works, *Ecumenical, Academic, and Pastoral Work, 1931–1932*, the editors state, "In sermon after sermon . . . Bonhoeffer sought to preach the gospel as concretely as possible . . . . For Bonhoeffer, concrete reality includes both the reality of God and the reality of the world. To ignore either the reality of God or the reality of the world leads to abstraction. Concrete reality is embodied in Jesus Christ, in his life, death, and resurrection. Certainly the Lutheran theology of the cross shaped his preaching. But for Bonhoeffer evangelical preaching was also shaped fully by the incarnation and the resurrection."

so that the genuineness of your faith—being more precious than gold that, though perishable, is tested by fire—may be found to result in praise and glory and honor when Jesus Christ is revealed. Although you have not seen him, you love him; and even though you do not see him now, you believe in him and rejoice with an indescribable and glorious joy, for you are receiving the outcome of your faith, the salvation of your souls.

This sermon is important to study because it becomes a baseline for Bonhoeffer's use of 1 Peter to support his life's work.

In the course of this homily, he is already working with the five themes we have just noted,[13] though he does not structure his sermon logically in the order of how he stated his five questions in 1942. Instead, he is guided by the flow of the text. Beginning the sermon with keying off of the paean of joy in verse 8, Bonhoeffer identifies joy as coterminous with a life lived with Christ. "Jesus Christ coming from God and returning to God . . . is the joy of God in the world, the joy of God catching fire in humanity, which is hungry for joy. . . . Just wait—and rejoice. He will come again."

But how, Bonhoeffer asks, can people rejoice when they have been abandoned? Here is where he makes use of 1 Peter's metaphor of the exile. His presentation is rather conventional, with the figure of the exile standing for displaced persons who are abandoned and homesick for their heavenly home, or, variously, as persons estranged from God. Nevertheless, his addition of the qualifiers "who are in barren, empty places, who don't know the way, who are alone," resonate with the historical moment of his experiencing negative exposure in confronting "the Jewish question."

The answer to the existential question: How can one rejoice when abandoned? comes with the realization that while our joy is real, the source of our joy cannot be comprehended. "But it is never what we can understand that brings us joy—it is that which we cannot understand but is true, real, and alive that sets us alight with joy." Here the second theme (confessing the source of one's strength outside oneself) makes its appearance. It is the joy of God in the world. Quoting from verse 8 again, Bonhoeffer offers the insight: "For you are allowed to love him whom you cannot see; you are allowed to believe in him who is lost to your sight. And nobody can take your love and your faith from you."

Analyzing his homiletical handing of the text, we see him blending the second theme of the incompressibility of joy with the fourth theme of

13. This sermon is found in Bonhoeffer, *Berlin, 1932–1933*, 466–71.

counter-intuitivity. This counter-intuitive construction is framed Christologically, which becomes the basis for the announcement of the fifth theme of endurance: "And nobody can take your love and your faith from you." In the context of the Reich's conference adoption of the *Führer* Principle his announcement must be appreciated as a criticism of Hitler. He uses verse 9 more conventionally, with its promise of salvation when Jesus returns, toward the end of the sermon to underscore this fifth theme of holding out.

The third theme of the calm demeanor makes its appearance mid-point in the sermon where Bonhoeffer gives it an instrumental cast. A calm demeanor is necessary for the reception of this special joy. "We have to become very quiet inwardly before we can even hear the soft sound of this word. Joy comes to life in the quiet and the mystery." This comment is a direct pastoral admonition which the text itself does not suggest, though it is supported by 1 Pet 5:7 ("Cast all your anxiety on him, because he cares for you").

Already it can be noticed that Bonhoeffer is moving away from any location of the source of joy in liberal, humanistic thought. Likewise, abandonment, in the sense of being an exile in one's own country, is a probable point of resonance, though the sermon continues to tread on traditional ground in the construal of sojourning as waiting for the Lord to return. Bonhoeffer will become much more focused on the experience of alienation as his struggle with the German Church and Nazism deepens. His muted criticism of the *Führer* Principle will also become stronger. As such, the sermon reflects the indeterminate situation of the church in Germany at the dawn of Nazism.

2. Manifesto to Our Brothers in the Ministry, Berlin-Dahlem, July 30, 1935[14]

By 1934, the situation in the German church was different. Bethge explains: "In 1932 there existed an unopposed established Church, but by 1934 the position had radically changed. Now . . . the Church found herself in a state of crisis."[15] In the intervening time, the Reich conference of German Christians and Hitler's installing a *Reichbischof* as his "confidential adviser and plenipotentiary in questions concerning the Protestant church"[16] provoked an upsurge of concerted opposition, known generally as the Confessing

---

14. Bonhoeffer, *Theological Education at Finkenwalde, 1935-1937*, 84–86.
15. Bonhoeffer, *Theological Education at Finkenwalde, 1935-1937*, 70.
16. Bethge, *Dietrich Bonhoeffer*, 270.

Church, out of which came the famous Barmen Declaration of 1934. Barmen, with its confession of *"solus Christos,"* gave the Confessing Church a fighting faith to resist the cries of *"solus* Adolf Hitler."[17] This declaration which dealt with theological convictions was followed soon by one in Dahlem which structured the forms and institutions of the Confessing Church in the Councils of Brethren.

A key development in the ongoing struggle was the establishment of a clandestine seminary independent of State supervision which would engage in the formation of ministers who would stand with Barmen, and to accomplish this, Bonhoeffer played an active role. The seminary of the Confessing Church began its operation in Zingst on April 26, 1935, and moved to Finkenwalde on June 24. During these critical months of the fledgling seminary, the State took further measures to isolate those who stood with Barmen and to harass further the school, already on precarious footing. Bonhoeffer responded by issuing a general statement to the influential group of Confessing Church ministers in Berlin where a text from 1 Peter plays a critical role.

The Manifesto frankly states that

> We believe that a new and perhaps the most difficult struggle is still to come for the church-community. All the recently implemented measures (finance departments, legislative authority, cost-sharing stipulations, establishment of the Ministry for Church Affairs with continued restrictions and expulsions) can be viewed only as intending to resolve the church question in *opposition* to *Barmen and Dahlem*. We must earnestly entreat the brothers to dispense with any interpretation of the church situation as harmless and to gird themselves with their congregations for the approaching decision. During the past few months we have experienced one disappointment after another while waiting for our church leadership to attain a decisive victory and state recognition of the Confessing Church. In the process, many of us have become tired and discouraged. We must confess that our own unbelief has seduced us into placing our hopes in human beings; and, indeed, have we not fostered and nourished such hopes both among ourselves and among others?

In his analysis of the crisis, Bonhoeffer frankly admits that "doubt and anxiety have made its nest among us, we lack clear guidance, our theological youth no longer knows whether it is jeopardizing its own future

---

17. Bethge, *Bonhoeffer, Exile and Martyr*, 70–71.

by pursuing its education, examination and ministry in the Confessing Church." Existence as an exile in one's own country is experienced as weakness, despair, discouragement, doubt, anxiety, and blindness, and finally impotence before the power of the State.

Bonhoeffer exhorts his church to renew its trust only in God in whom to put one's hope. He rivets this point into his manifesto by quoting 1 Pet 1:13, "Therefore prepare your minds for action, discipline yourselves, set all your hope on the grace that Jesus Christ will bring you when he is revealed." The verse becomes a pivot point to move the manifesto from criticism to consolation, as Bonhoeffer implores, "Let us not lose heart because the future of the church is shrouded in impenetrable darkness as far as our own vision is concerned." In the most difficult struggle still to come for the church-community, "What we have been commanded is first and foremost to ensure in our own ministry and in our own church-community *that the Confessing Church lies solely from the word, from grace, and from faith.*" He concludes, "*Christ is the one consolation that will be left to us.*"

This Manifesto illustrates how Bonhoeffer, when under severe stress of facing no good options, appeals utterly to power outside himself not to extricate him from this situation but to undergird preparing himself to meet the challenge facing him. This is the substance of consolation which can be gained by a confessional handling of scripture. He describes eloquently a basic counter-intuitive strategy growing out of this consolation in a sermon on Psalm 42 which he preached to seminarians at Zingst the month before on June 2.[18]

> Yet I will confess God before all the world and before all the enemies of God when in the most profound tribulation I believe in God's goodness, when in guilt I believe in forgiveness, when in death I believe in life, when in defeat I believe in victory and when in abandonment I believe in God's gracious presence. Those who have found God in the cross of Jesus Christ know how wondrously God is concealed in this world, and how in fact God is closest to us precisely when we think God is farthest away.

---

18 Bonhoeffer, *Theological Education at Finkenwalde, 1935-1937*, 850-53.

3. Standing Strong in Babylon, Revelation 14:6–13, Finkenwalde, Remembrance Sunday, November 24, 1935[19]

Revelation 14:6–11 shares with 1 Peter a potent symbol, Babylon. "Your sister church in Babylon, chosen together with you, sends you greetings; and so does my son Mark" (1 Pet 5:13). While there is no surviving evidence of Bonhoeffer's use of the Petrine text, his sermon from Revelation may function as a supportive text to 1 Peter. The sermon also is another occasion for Bonhoeffer to reflect more deeply on the status of being an exile in one's own country. Bonhoeffer activates the symbol of Babylon in his bitter opposition to an attempt by Christians in the German state church to undermine his seminarian's commitment to the affirmations of the Confessing Church. Some preparatory explanation is necessary.

In the Manifesto just considered, Bonhoeffer frankly admits that "doubt and anxiety have made its nest among us, we lack clear guidance, our theological youth no longer knows whether it is jeopardizing its own future by pursuing its education, examination and ministry in the Confessing Church." He was referring to the ploy of the German Christians in Berlin to offer "legalization" to Confessing Church seminarians. If they agreed to take their theological examination under the German Christian-led examination committees, they would be given financial and job security. This was a very attractive offer, and in late 1935 and early 1936 some were beginning to consider "legalization."[20] The mounting allure on the Confessing Church was very much on Bonhoeffer's mind and heart as he channeled his bitter opposition to the German church and his pastoral zeal for his seminarians into the exploration of the meaning of Babylon.

By the first century CE, Babylon was securely fixed as a symbol of the seductiveness of imperial power, as well as its eventual collapse.[21] First century Christians used the content of this symbol to refer to the Roman Empire as illustrated in Rev 14:8, "Then another angel, a second, followed, saying, 'Fallen, fallen is Babylon the great! She has made all nations drink of the wine of the wrath of her fornication.'"

In Bonhoeffer's situation, his homiletical employment of this symbol communicates with passion and fearlessness his bitter opposition to the pressures of the German Church upon his seminarians.

---

19. Barrett, *The Collected Sermons*, 159–68.
20. See Barrett, *The Collected Sermons*, 160.
21. See, among others, Ackroyd, *Exile and Restoration*, 247.

> That is what John saw—but he also saw that Babylon was still great, powerful, and bursting with strength—that Babylon was still standing there, invincible in the world, and that all people were trembling before it, falling to their knees—Babylon, the enemy of God—the city that never stops building its tower up into heaven—Babylon, which on its own power defies Christ, the crucified Lord, which intoxicates people with its glittering and tempting vices, as a prostitute intoxicates her lovers with heavy wine—which befuddles and confuses and courts people with all sorts of splendor and godless grandeur—Babylon, which human beings love, around which they flock, into whose nets they senselessly stumble—Babylon, which demands nothing of its subjects except blind love and intoxication, which it also abundantly and extravagantly showers on them, things the human heart and its wild desire lust after—who would dare say that this Babylon is not eternal?—it will take a bad fall—woe to it!

Then, in a seamless move, Bonhoeffer pivots to draw a tighter circle of threat, beginning with a frank acknowledgement of being the exile in one's own country.

> *How anxiously the Christian community*—which neither can nor wants to be a citizen of this city, a community that must dwell and suffer on the periphery, outside this city—how anxiously must it be watching that city, how fervently must it be interceding in prayer, how often must it have yearned in prayer for its fall!—Who is Babylon—was it Rome? Where is it today? Even today we still do not dare say—not out of fear of human beings! instead the church-community simply does not yet know—though it does see terrible things and disclosures approaching.

In the midst of the concentric contexts of the allure of Babylon and tightening the noose around the exilic church, Bonhoeffer moves directly to pastoral encouragement:

> [A]nd now—a voice from heaven, the message of joy for the community of believers—"fallen is Babylon the great . . . everything has already been completed, God has already passed judgment, Babylon already does not even exist—Babylon cannot endure—because it cannot endure before God. Hence: *do not fear* Babylon, it has no power over you—it has already been judged—it is all merely dust and smoke and ruins—do not take it *so deadly seriously* anymore, do not let your *hatred* and *zealousness consume* you, for it is all so temporary, so temporary—it is *not even important*

anymore—other things, however, are indeed important—remain firm in faith, hold fast to Christ, do not be touched by Babylon, remain sober, and do let fear overwhelm you—listen to God's voice, the Almighty, who says: fallen is Babylon the great. That alone is important—that alone leads to life—those who fall prey to Babylon, however, also fall prey to death and judgment—Fallen is Babylon, rejoice, O community of believers!

Within this extended peroration, four of the questions which Bonhoeffer frames in 1942–43 are powerfully exposited: the exile in one's native land, the appeal to remain calm and confident in the face of both temptation and a looming terror, the definitive intervention from outside the crisis, and the assurance from God that you can endure. While Bonhoeffer may have preferred the text in Revelation over 1 Peter, because of its more extensive development of the symbol of Babylon, signs in the sermon strongly suggest that the two books were mutually supportive in the creation of this sermon. This is particularly evident in his treatment of Rev 14:7 "Fear God, and give him glory" with 1 Pet 2:17 "Fear God, honor the emperor" and 5:8 "Discipline yourselves, keep alert. Like a roaring lion your adversary the devil prowls around, looking for someone to devour."

4. Confirmation Instruction Plan, October 19–23, 1936[22]

A major aspect of Bonhoeffer's struggle with the deteriorating situation in his country took place in context of ecumenical relations. In 1936 these discussions focused on the competition between various German Christian groups to gain recognition and standing in the World Council of Churches.[23] An important conference in Chamby, Switzerland, August 21, 1936, which representatives of the major church groups in Germany attended, further solidified the isolation of the Confessing Church and deepened Bonhoeffer's conviction that his church would have to take additional measures to preserve its distinctive witness against Nazism.

To give theological grounding to the witness of the Confessing Church, Bonhoeffer wrote a Confirmation Instruction Plan and introduced it into the course work of the Finkenwalde seminary. He shared this catechism for

---

22. Bohoeffer, *Theological Education at Finkenwalde, 1935–1937*, 782–811.

23. Much has been written about his relations with the Anglican Bishop J. K. Bell throughout the war years. See, Bethge, *Dietrich Bonhoeffer*.

the first time at a retreat October 19, 1936, which brought together students who had studied with him in the second session (1935–36) at Finkenwalde with those who were beginning the fourth session.

While he wrote in the form of a classical catechism, he intended this document to be specifically for the Confessing Church. For example, in the exposition of the Apostles' Creed, the question: "Which is the proper church of Christ to which you belong?" requires the answer "It is the Confessing Church in Germany." A later question: "On which is this church based?" attracts the answer: "Our church is based solely on the Word of God in the Holy Scriptures. The Holy Spirit has also given our church an evangelical exposition of Scripture and a testimony of faith in the confessional writings of the Reformation and of the Barmen Synod."[24]

The particularity of this catechism is starkly revealed in subsequent entries on how the church expresses its character in the harsh realities of the present moment. This is where Bonhoeffer pairs the content of his answers with 1 Peter.[25] He begins by describing the character of the church in terms of what God has promised it: "The Lord Jesus has promised that [the church] will have to suffer persecution and the cross in discipleship to him. But he also promised it the perfect blessedness of fellowship and eternal victory." The question immediately following asks: "How does the church-community bear this suffering?" Its answer shows the clear impression of 1 Peter: "It is not surprised, and it is not ashamed. Instead it rejoices in the company of its Lord. It knows that its cross is a sign of victory. Wherever one suffers, all suffer." Textual roots to this answer are cited as 1 Pet 4:1 ("Since therefore Christ suffered in the flesh, arm yourselves with the same intention") and 12–19 (which begins "Beloved do not be surprised at the fiery ordeal that is taking place among you"). The next question asks: "How does the church-community live in the world?" Again, 1 Peter provides important vocabulary for the answer: "It lives as an alien that is sojourning home. It uses only those goods of the world that it needs. Its heart is not in this world but in heaven." In addressing readers as aliens citations of 1 Pet 1:1 ("To the exiles of the Dispersion") and 2:11 ("Beloved, I urge you as aliens and exiles") are included.

Recalling the demonstration in chapter 1 that the epistle writer drew upon conventional language in advising readers not to be surprised and ashamed as a way of consoling them in the contest of fiery trials, we note

---

24. Bethge, *Dietrich Bonhoeffer*, 806.
25. Bethge, *Dietrich Bonhoeffer*, 808.

how the ancient language spoke to Bonhoeffer as he counseled the "aliens" of his Confessing Church. Also worth noting is his citing 1 Pet 4:12–19 with its double meaning of the cross to support a long-standing strategy of living counter-intuitively. The figure of the alien is central, though Bonhoeffer emphasizes its other-worldly direction. Nevertheless, as will become evident in subsequent entries, Bonhoeffer makes the figure of the alien increasingly bear the experience of being a stranger in one's own land.

The emphasis on being an alien in the exigencies of the present appear in the catechism in entries concerning the relationships of the church and worldly authorities. Again, 1 Peter strongly informs the answers. To the question: "What does the church-community do for the worldly authorities?" the answer indicates how 1 Pet 2:12–17 (which begins "Conduct yourselves honorably among the Gentiles") has shaped the experience as an alien in the gritty reality of struggle: "[The church-community] obeys [the authorities] to the point of offering one's own bodily life; it is a model of honorable life; it prays for them; it preaches the truth of the gospel to the people." The following three verses from the source text (1 Pet 2:18–20) provide the shaping of the answer to a following question: "What is the church-community's position toward unjust authorities?" Here the painful requirements of living as an alien are plainly laid out: "The church-community performs without fear the work to which the Lord has commissioned it. It obeys God more than it does human beings [see 1 Pet 2:17]. It willingly suffers all punishment and prays for its persecutors."

Thus, texts from 1 Peter buttress entries in the Confirmation Instruction Plan which are aligned with three of the five major themes Bonhoeffer lays down in his 1942–43 summation: the experience of being an exile in one's own land, the strategy of counter-intuitive living, and endurance.

5. *The Cost of Discipleship*, 1937[26]

Two events occurred in 1937 that mark a decisive turn in Bonhoeffer's leadership in the increasingly isolated Confessing Church. The first is the closing of the preachers seminary in Finkenwalde by the Gestapo in September and the second is the publication of *The Cost of Discipleship* in November. While the two are not related in terms of cause and effect, the manuscript of *Discipleship* having been completed by July, they are mutually illuminating. The

---

26. Found in Bonhoeffer, *Discipleship*.

book is a major work oriented around the Sermon on the Mount, so it may be expected that 1 Peter plays a minor role in its overall objective.

Nevertheless, Bonhoeffer has the opportunity to develop in chapter 11 the image of the sojourner/alien which he had sketched in the Confirmation Instruction Plan the preceding year, and 1 Peter continues to be a pivotal source. In a carefully structured paragraph the alien's status is circumscribed from both other-worldly as well as this-worldly viewpoints.[27] Then the two images of the alien are constructively placed in counter-intuitive tension. This progression is repeated twice in the paragraph. The following table displays an analysis of these two thought patterns by reading down the second and third columns on this and the following page.

A present day determination of the sojourner	Christians are poor and suffering, hungry and thirsty, gentle, compassionate and peaceable, persecuted and scorned by the world.	They are strangers and sojourners on this earth (Heb. 11:13; 13:14; 1 Peter 1:1).
A future oriented determination of the sojourner	At any moment it may receive the signal to move on. Then it will break camp, leaving behind all worldly friends and relatives, and following only the voice of the one who has called it. It leaves the foreign country and moves onward toward its heavenly home.	They set their minds on things that are above, not on things that are of the earth (Col 3:2).

27. Bonhoeffer, *Discipleship*, 225

| A counter-intuitive faithful life | Yet it is for their sake alone that the world is still preserved. They shield the world from God's judgment of wrath. They suffer so that the world can still live under God's forbearance. | For their true life has not yet been revealed; it is still hidden with Christ in God (Col 3:3). They are still hidden even from themselves. The left hand does not know what the right hand is doing. As a visible church-community, their own identity remains completely invisible to them. They look only to their Lord. He is in heaven, and their life for which they are waiting is in him. But when Christ, their life, reveals himself, then they will also be revealed with him in glory (Col 3:4). |

The opportunity for constructive thinking yields two powerful traits which become critical tools in the counter-intuitive life of the alien. Suffering has two sides to it. First, there is the hard reality of human pain shown to the world. This is placed against the value of suffering as substitutionary atonement which is informed by a theology of the Cross. The hard reality of suffering shown to the world actually has the purpose of alleviating the crisis of the present world under the certainty of God's judgement. The suffering of the alien becomes vicarious suffering for the world. As such it merges with the vicarious suffering of Christ. Bonhoeffer will develop this insight more broadly in his major biblical study on temptation to be examined in the following extract.

It is possible that Bonhoeffer saw the point of this suffering as "buying time" until the present situation could be altered. More likely, with his description of the alien, Bonhoeffer was laying the groundwork for a new understanding of martyrdom. His biographer, Bethge, identifies Bonhoeffer's description of suffering for the sake of the life of the world as a new kind of martyrdom. "Whereas formerly martyrdom was the result of bearing testimony to the name of Jesus Christ in a hostile world, now martyrdom is often the result of bearing testimony on behalf of a threatened '*humanum*', it has become a sacrifice for the sake of humanity."[28]

The second trait underscores the quality of unknowing, even disorientation, that besets the alien's vocation as a bearer of substitutionary atonement. This trait takes life from the realities of pointlessness, fluidity, lack of control, and isolation with which someone must contend who suffers for the sake of the care of a world in which they are an alien. Bonhoeffer points out not only the public shame and misunderstanding of the individual which leads to physical and psychological isolation, but also the disappearance of the church-community into a discredited incognito ("As a visible church-community, their own identity remains completely invisible to them.").[29] Only one avenue points a way towards the stamina required to live at this extreme stage: the church-community's steadfast lock on Christ on whom the alien risks utter trust for an eschatological resolution. A possible subtext for this counter-intuitive solution is 1 Pet 1:8–9 ("Although you have not seen him, you love him, and even though you do not see him now, you believe in him and rejoice with an indescribable and glorious joy") even though Bonhoeffer does not cite it.

Bethge gives the name "blessed alienation" to living as an alien in one's native land: "the 'chosen one' finds his identity and his purpose when he recognizes the call to the strange land and follows it. At first the called one scarcely knows how he will continue to live, but then he learns that he gave up his home so that he could home within himself greater and completely new and different things."[30]

6. Bible Study on Temptation, June 20–25, 1938[31]

The context for this piece of extended theological reflection has both ecclesiastical and political aspects. On March 12, 1938, Germany annexed Austria in the *Anschluss*. The wave of enthusiasm produced in Germany

---

28. Bethge, *Bonhoeffer, Exile and Martyr*, 158.

29. Bethge, describing the martyrdom of the alien for the sake of a justified "*humanum*" remarks perceptively, "And when their martyrdom came to pass, it did so in the twilight of political conspiracy, and under the stifling feeling that their effort had come too late. Certainly it did not lead to a public confession in the market-place or the Colosseum, nor any obviously heroic notice. Everything took place in the silent incognito of concentration camps and dark cellars." *Bonhoeffer, Exile and Martyr*, 162–63.

30. Bethge, *Bonhoeffer, Exile and Martyr*, 114.

31. Bonhoeffer, *Theological Education Underground*, 386–414.

was seized upon by Reich church authorities to pressure German pastors to take the loyalty oath to Hitler as *Führer*. On April 20, 1938, an order was published in the *Legal Gazette* "that all pastors in active office were to take the oath of allegiance to the *Führer*."[32] The oath stated: "I swear that I will be faithful and obedient to Adolf Hitler, the *Führer* of the German Reich and people, that I will conscientiously observe the laws and carry out the duties of my office, so help me God."[33] The following four months were fraught with ecclesiastical conferences where matters of conscience provoked by swearing this oath were exhaustively discussed. Conditions which were patently theologically bankrupt were proposed under which the oath could be taken. This ploy eased the troubled consciences of pastors, and many took the oath. The capitulating of the church to Hitler was a crushing blow to Bonhoeffer.

In this setting of extreme state pressure on German pastors, Bonhoeffer in June convened a reunion of seminarians from Finkenwalde at Zingst where he shared an extensive Bible study on temptation. While this study is centered on the synoptic accounts of the temptation of Christ, Bonhoeffer ranges throughout the New Testament in developing his subject. We will limit our consideration to how 1 Peter contributes to the project.

It is clear that Bonhoeffer intended to place the synoptic accounts of Jesus' temptation in conversation with the fiery trials of 1 Peter. He chose 1 Pet 4:12–19 to lay down a base for what is probably the most complex theological thinking of the Bible study.[34]

> Beloved, do not be surprised at the fiery ordeal that is taking place among you to test you, as though something strange were happening to you. But rejoice insofar as you are sharing Christ's sufferings, so that you may also be glad and shout for joy when his glory is revealed. If you are reviled for the name of Christ, you are blessed, because the spirit of glory, which is the Spirit of God, is resting on you. But let none of you suffer as a murderer, a thief, a criminal, or even as a mischief maker. Yet if any of you suffers as a Christian, do not consider it a disgrace, but glorify God because you bear this name. For the time has come for judgment to begin with the household of God; if it begins with us, what will be the end for those who do not obey the gospel of God? And

---

32. Bethge, *Dietrich Bonhoeffer*, 599.
33. Bethge, *Dietrich Bonhoeffer*, 600.
34. Bonhoeffer, *Theological Education Underground*, 407–9.

> "If it is hard for the righteous to be saved,
> what will become of the ungodly and the sinners?"
>
> Therefore, let those suffering in accordance with God's will entrust themselves to a faithful Creator, while continuing to do good.

Bonhoeffer describes the "fiery trial" (v. 12) his colleagues are encountering: "A suffering that is foreign to the world, the *suffering for the sake of the Lord Jesus Christ*." He points out that for the righteous person to "suffer *for the sake of his own righteousness* may easily become a stumbling block for one who believes in Jesus Christ." While general suffering may be unavoidable,

> suffering for the sake of Christ could immediately find an end with the denial of Christ.... And precisely here Satan has an open field for his activities. He incites the yearnings of the flesh for happiness and turns the Christian's own pious insights against him, by pointing out the folly and godlessness of voluntary suffering as well as the pious way out, the special solution to his conflicts.... [This presents a] genuine temptation toward apostasy.

Here Bonhoeffer may be thinking of the servile compromises the Confessing Church created to alleviate troubled consciences of German pastors who signed the oath of allegiance to Hitler.

At this point of greatest pressure to become apostate, Bonhoeffer appeals to the counter-intuitive strategy of 1 Peter.

> The Christian should not be surprised about this temptation but rather understand that precisely here he is led into the communion of the sufferings of Jesus Christ (1 Pet 4:13). Even here, Satan's temptation pushes the Christian again into the arms of Jesus Christ, the Crucified One. Precisely where Satan robs a human being of his own freedom and leads it against Christ, the Christian's bond with Jesus Christ will become most gloriously visible.

"What does it mean to be in communion with the sufferings of Christ?" Bonhoeffer asks. "In the first place, it means *joy* (1 Pet 4:13). It means *recognition of the innocence* where the Christian suffers as a Christian (v. 15). It means *the honor of God* in the name by which I am called a Christian (v. 16)." These markers, produced by this counter-intuitive strategy, are the seed-bed for new agency for the alien.

His probing into the implications of suffering with Christ reaches its most complex level when he proceeds to ask: "How can the suffering that I experience precisely as a Christian, *as a justified one*, be at the same time understood as a *judgment* passed on sin?" Here is where Bonhoeffer uses the answer to this question to delineate suffering with Christ from two types of suffering with which it is liable to be confused: suffering as fanaticism and suffering for the sake of a hero or ethical ideal. Bonhoeffer quotes without citing 1 Pet 4:17 to anchor his discussion. "For the time has come for judgment to begin with the household of God." We look at each of these distinctions.

It is God's judgment contained in suffering for the sake of Jesus that saves suffering from being mere fanaticism. God's judgment gives a point to suffering with Christ by seeing Christ's suffering as

> God's *only* judgment that came over Christ and that will come in the end over all flesh, namely, God's judgment over sin. No one can stand on Christ's side without also partaking in this judgment by God, for here lies the difference between Christ and the world in that he bore the judgment that is despised and shaken off by the world.

Therefore, to suffer with Christ is to join him in suffering for the world's sake. What the world itself will not acknowledge, the church is to suffer vicariously for the *humanum*. Here Bonhoeffer carries forward insights he previously created in his use of 1 Peter in *Cost of Discipleship*.

This is also the basis for the difference between suffering in communion with Jesus Christ and suffering in the community of some ethical ideal or political hero. The Christian recognizes the guilt of the world bound up in Jesus that must be borne and endured in suffering with Christ. "In this way the Christian's suffering of judgment in communion with Jesus Christ becomes a vicarious suffering for the world" which is the opposite of suffering with a political hero. Bonhoeffer appeals to 1 Peter to underpin this point: "So judgment beginning at the house of God [1 Pet 4:17] is God's gracious judgment over Christians followed by the last judgment in God's wrath on the ungodly." In the Christian's communion with the cross of Christ with its double-sided meaning of vicarious suffering of judgment and opening the way to salvation, the Christian sojourner/alien brings about vicariously God's grace for the world.

Recalling the five central questions Bonhoeffer raised in his essay "After Ten Years" it is evident that they are all contained in this complex theological passage: the special experience of exile as alienation from one's native state, the appeal to a source of strength outside the human condition, a deep sense of confidence in pursuing the hard path, the counter-intuitive strategy of engagement, and the reality of being able to endure.

His study on temptation marks a turn in reorienting Bonhoeffer' construal of the sojourner/alien away from the perspective of the future. Now, future orientation is not focused on an otherworldly longing but on the exile/alien's proleptic suffering of the future judgment of God *in this world*. In suffering with Jesus, the exile sees personal suffering as actually bearing God's judgment on the world in a vicarious way. Thus the one experiencing alienation from home and state actually serves their native land by opening up the possibility of a new future for the world beyond judgment. This insight found its way into his 1942–43 summation, "After Ten Years": "Or rather, facing a great historical turning point, did the responsible thinkers of another generation ever feel differently than we do today—precisely because something genuinely new was forming that was not yet apparent in the existing alternatives?" Bonhoeffer's turn to a this-worldly playing out of an other-worldly determination is clearly expressed in his 1939 "Meditation on Ps 119" when he comments on "I am a guest on earth; do not take your commandments from me" (v. 19):

> I may not evade my destiny to be a guest and a stranger, and thereby God's call into this sojourner status, by dreaming away my earthly life with thoughts about heaven. There is a very godless homesickness for the other world that will certainly not be stilled by a homecoming. I am meant to be a guest, with all this entails. I should not close my heart apathetically to the tasks, pains, and joys of the earth, and I should wait patiently for the divine promise to be redeemed, but truly wait for it, and not rob myself of it in advance, in wishes and dreams. Nothing is said here about the homeland itself. I know that it cannot be this earth, yet I know nonetheless that the earth is God's and that I am already on this earth not just as a guest of the earth but as a pilgrim and a sojourner (Ps. 39:13). But because I am nothing on earth but a guest, without rights, without support, without security, because God himself has made me so weak and lowly, therefore, he has given me one single firm pledge for my goal: his word. This one certainty will not be withdrawn from me; God will keep this word and through it will let me feel his strength. Wherever the word of home is with me, I will find my way in the strange land; I will find my rights in the midst of injustice,

my support in the midst of insecurity, my strength in my work, patience in the midst of suffering.[35]

The wrestling with suffering described in this piece and the one previously can be summarized in five theses:

1. The ends of suffering are changed by the identification of the sufferer with the crucified-resurrected Christ. Under this identification, suffering releases a new future for the *humanum*.

2. The conditions causing suffering do not change, but their intended result is absorbed in and ultimately transformed by the crucified-resurrected Christ.

3. The one who is suffering must negotiate both the intended goal of the suffering as well as the new one given in the crucified-resurrected Christ.

4. This requires constant inscribing the new goal in the suffering one's person. This requirement underscores the crucial necessity of worship as the space of inscribing.

5. Because of the new goal of suffering, the fiery trial does not hobble resistance/counter-behavior, no matter how feeble, and a steady, if faltering, dignity and hopeful outlook can be maintained.

Bonhoeffer's systematic way of coping with the fiery trial by pointing suffering in the world towards God's gracious redemption of the world has a formal similarity to the way Liebengood employs a "plan" to answer the question of continual suffering after Christ's resurrection. Moreover, Bonhoeffer's establishment of an asymmetry of suffering not leading to dishonor but to new creation anticipates Holloway's schema of survival by Disidentification.

7. Letter to Eberhard Bethge, November 18, 1943[36]

The next occurrence of Bonhoeffer's reaching for 1 Peter comes in 1943. During the intervening years, he had briefly come to America only to return to Germany where he became involved in the conspiracy to assassinate

---

35. Bonhoeffer, *Theological Education Underground, 1937-1940*. 522. Bonhoeffer called this his favorite psalm. See Bethge, *Dietrich Bonhoeffer*, 661.

36. Bonhoeffer, *Letters and Papers*, 178–80.

Hitler. This involved considerable travel and clandestine work with the ecumenical church. In April 1943, following failed attempts to assassinate Hitler, he was arrested along with other co-conspirators, and sent to Tegel prison. He truly was an alien in his own country.

The shock of prison was devastating. In a letter to Bethge, striking for the way Bonhoeffer exposed his vulnerable spirit, he writes of how during the first twelve days at Tegel, "I was kept isolated and treated as a dangerous criminal—to this day the cells on either side of mine are occupied almost exclusively by death-row prisoners in chains." His sense of isolation only intensified by the withdrawal of spiritual support for many long months "without worship, confession, and the Lord's Supper and without *consolation fratrum*." In a rare moment of vulnerability, he pours out his heart to Bethge, "[M]y pastor once more, as you have so often been in the past . . . listen to me . . . . You are the only person who knows that 'acedia'-'tristitia' with its ominous consequences has often haunted me, and you perhaps worried about me in this respect—so I feared at the time."[37]

Bonhoeffer is clearly referring to wresting with severe temptation [*Anfechtung*]. In the accompanying notes to this letter an explanation of *Anfechtung* gives it a broader meaning than the English word "temptation." "*Anfechtung* includes the idea of a person being lured to act against God's will, but it also denotes 'tribulation' in the sense of being assaulted by the powers of darkness." *Acedia* is a form of *Anfechtung* in which "*a person disintegrates internally . . . .* Everything is meaningless, everything completely dark between the person and God, so that the person loses God altogether." *Tristitia* has a wide range of meanings including sadness, grief, melancholy, and sorrow.

Here Bonhoeffer offers a graphic description of the existential "fiery trial" which has beset him. He is happy to report to Bethge that "Paul Gerhardt [the hymn writer] proved of value in unimagined ways, as well as the Psalms and Revelation. I was preserved in those days from all severe temptations [*Anfechtungen*]." However, he shares with Bethge a more specific example of *Anfechtung* he encountered in the beginning of his imprisonment:

---

37. Bonhoeffer expresses similar thoughts to his parents soon after he was imprisoned in a letter May 13, 1943, "I have never understood as clearly as I have here what the Bible and Luther mean by "temptation" [*Anfechgtung*]. The peace and serenity by which one had been carried are suddenly shaken without any apparent physical or psychological reason, and the heart becomes, as Jeremiah very aptly put it, an obstinate and anxious thing that one is unable to fathom. One experiences this as an attack from the outside, as evil powers that seek to rob one of what is most essential." *Letters and Papers*, 78.

"the question also plagued me as to whether it is really the cause of Christ for whose sake I have inflicted such distress on all of you." Here is where he reaches again to 1 Peter to push "this thought out of my head as a *Anfechtung* and [I] became certain that my task was precisely the endurance of such a boundary situation with all its problematic elements, and became quite happy with this and have remained so to this day. 1 Pet. 2:20; 3:14."[38]

Significantly, in his hour of greatest need, Bonhoeffer reaches for 1 Peter and finds two citations which help him understand himself as functioning faithfully in a boundary situation. The first citation reads, "But if you endure when you do right and suffer for it, you have God's approval." The following verses anchor this counter-intuitive strategy firmly in the believer's union with Christ: "For to this you have been called, because Christ also suffered for you, leaving you an example, so that you should follow in his steps . . . he entrusted himself to the one who judges justly." The second citation reads similarly: "But even if you suffer for doing what is right, you are blessed. Do not fear what they fear, and do not be intimidated." Both citations help Bonhoeffer to "read" himself, as well as calling him back to place utter trust in God. The texts anchor a person's enduring the boundary situation, with all its problematic elements, inside the company of the suffering Christ. The upshot of this linkage is an attitude of contentment, resoluteness, and satisfaction. Out of this attitude, possibilities for new agency emerge.

The term "boundary situation" functions as a technical term that names Bonhoeffer's living on the edge between what is seen and what is undercover. While he may have used this to refer to his clandestine work, his citing of texts in 1 Peter show that the boundary now centers on his life that is hidden in Christ. Bonhoeffer first encountered the term as a student reading Paul Tillich in 1931–32 where his notes record, "It is at the boundaries of our existence that [according to Tillich], we experience the radical No; if we accept this boundary situation we find ourselves affirmed. In recognizing that we are sinners, in essence we already have the recognition of mercy." Bonhoeffer disagrees with Tillich's construal, thinking that it preempts, by our own power, God's act of grace. He sets down his correction as follows: "When the No turns to a Yes, that is of course an act of God in complete freedom and is not based on the No. It is God who must

---

38. In his letter to parents, Bonhoeffer states his strategy of endurance, "What matters is being focused on what one still has and what can be done—and that is still a great deal—and on restraining within oneself the rising thoughts about what one cannot do and the inner restlessness and resentment about the entire situation." *Letters and Papers*, 78.

overcome God's own No and become angry at God's own anger (Luther); [this is] the reason for the cross."[39]

A contrast can be drawn between the construal of the boundary between 1931–32 and 1943. Initially, the boundary situation for Bonhoeffer ran between No and Yes, between judgment and grace. It was a boundary at which we are all thrown upon the mercy of God to act in complete freedom, where "God must become angry at God's own anger." By 1943 "boundary" had become the way Bonhoeffer named the pattern for authentic Christian existence.[40] At the boundary between reality and deception he joined the conspiracy to kill Hitler as a situational act of righteousness.[41] The path he took toward that boundary began with forming his life around the counterintuitive strategy of Jesus, based on utter trust in God.

The boundary as the place for witness and action is a notion that comes to light in his prison writings. As such, it has all the marks of thoughtful reflection. While he does not describe the steps he took to arrive at this way of naming his situation, it is safe to assume, given his life in prison, that intense wrestling with the example of Jesus in the text of 1 Peter played a major role. We are fortunate that he shares his experience of intense study with the text in a circular letter to his Finkenwalde former students March 1, 1943.

> For me the daily silent reflection on the word of God as it applies to me—even if only for a few minutes—tends to become the crystallization of all that brings inner and outer order to my life. With the interruption and dissolution of our previously ordered life that the present age has brought about—with the danger of losing our inner order through the profusion of events, through the all-consuming claims of work and service, through doubts and moral conflicts [*Anfechtung*] battle and unrest of all kinds—meditation gives our life something like constancy. It preserves the connection with our former life, from baptism through confirmation to ordination; it sustains us in the healing community of the congregation, of the brothers, of the spiritual home; it is a spark of the hearth fire that the congregations at home want to tend for you; it is a fountain of peace, of patience, and of joy; it is like a magnet directing all the available powers for ordering our life toward its pole; it is like pure deep water in which the heavens with their

---

39. Bonhoeffer, *Ecumenical, Academic, and Pastoral Work*, 237.
40. See Bethge, *Bonhoeffer, Exile and Martyr*, 130.
41. Bethge, *Bonhoeffer, Exile and Martyr*, 115.

clouds and sun are radiantly mirrored. But it also serves the Most High, in that it opens for God a space of discipline and quiet, of healing order and contentment. Do we not all have a deep longing, however unacknowledged, for such a gift?[42]

8. Daily Text Meditation for June 7 and 8, 1944[43]

A sample of this meditative work is the last extant example of Bonhoeffer's use of 1 Peter, which is found in his reflections on Ps 34:19 ("Many are the afflictions of the righteous; but the LORD rescues them from them all"), coupled with 1 Pet 3:9 ("Do not repay evil for evil or abuse for abuse; but, on the contrary, repay with a blessing. It is for this that you were called—that you might inherit a blessing"). By way of summary to this chapter we will display the course of the meditation in a table format based on the five questions that animate his 1942–43 essay "After Ten Years." Whether intentionally or not, Bonhoeffer writes his meditation in the order of how he stated his five questions which are stated in the first column. The second column displays the key thought of what he wrote. The third column contains his elaboration of that thought.

---

42. Bonhoeffer, *Conspiracy and Imprisonment*, 253–55.
43. Bonhoeffer, *Conspiracy and Imprisonment*, 629–33.

Question from "After Ten Years"	Key Thought in Meditation	Comment
Have there ever been people in history who in their time, like us, had so little ground under their feet, people to whom every possible alternative open to them at the time appeared equally unbearable, senseless, and contrary to life?	The righteous suffer from the world, the unrighteous do not.	The righteous suffer from things that others take for granted and consider essential. The righteous suffer from unrighteousness, from the meaninglessness and perversion of world events; they suffer from the destruction of the divine orders of marriage and the family. They suffer from this not only because these things represent for them a deprivation but also because they recognize in them something ungodly. The world says: that is just how it is; it will always be that way and must be so. The righteous say: it should not be that way; it is against God. This is the chief hallmark by which the righteous can be recognized, that they suffer in this way. To some extent they bring into the world God's own way of perceiving things; that is why they suffer just as God suffers at the hands of the world.

Question from "After Ten Years"	Key Thought in Meditation	Comment
Have there been those who like us looked for the source of their strength beyond all those available alternatives? Were they looking entirely in what has passed away and in what is yet to come?	But the Lord rescues them.	God's help is not found in all human suffering. But in the suffering of the righteous God's help is always present, because the righteous suffer with God. God is always there. The righteous know that God allows them to suffer in this way [so that] they learn to love God for God's own sake. In suffering the righteous find God. That is their help. If you find God in your separation, you are finding help.
And, nevertheless, without being dreamers, did they await with calm and confidence the successful outcome of their endeavor?	The response of the righteous to the suffering that the world inflicts on them is: to bless.	That was God's response to the world that nailed Christ to the cross: blessing. God does not repay evil for evil, and thus the righteous should not do so either. No judgment, no abuse, but blessing. The world would have no hope if this were not the case. The world lives by the blessing of God and of the righteous and thus has a future. Blessing means laying one's hand on something and saying: Despite everything, you belong to God.

Question from "After Ten Years"	Key Thought in Meditation	Comment
		This is what we do with the world that inflicts such suffering on us. We do not abandon it; we do not repudiate, despise, or condemn it. Instead we call it back to God, we give it hope, we lay our hand on it and say: may God's blessing come upon you, may God renew you; be blessed, world created by God, you who belong to your Creator and Redeemer.
Or rather, facing a great historical turning point, did the responsible thinkers of another generation ever feel differently than we do today—precisely because something genuinely new was forming that was not yet apparent in the existing alternatives?		We have received God's blessing in happiness and in suffering. Yet those who have been blessed can do nothing but pass on this blessing; indeed, they must be a blessing wherever they are. The world can [be] renewed only by the impossible, [and] the impossible is the blessing of God.
Who Stands Firm?		

The hermeneutical pathway marked by the five questions undergirds the natural flow of the meditation. Words keyed to the final question Who Stands Firm? are absent in the meditation. However, this is supplied in the closing words of an accompanying note to his dear friends Eberhard and Renate Bethge. "These words flowed onto paper when, thinking of you, I meditated on the daily texts for the days that await you. They are merely thrown together in haste and not formulated in advance and are intended only to accompany you in your own reading of the texts and if possible to help a little. . . . Now farewell, be fully confident, and hope along with me that we may see one another again soon! Your Dietrich."

In characteristic fashion, Bonhoeffer shows that the power of scripture is to engender confidence. Furthermore, this meditation allows Bonhoeffer to employ a powerful description of a Christian's suffering as someone who bears what breaks God's heart and yet finds from the same God an inner resource to bless the world, the *humanum*. This is redemptive suffering.

9. Final meditation on Isaiah 53:5 and 1 Peter 1:3

On Sunday, April 8, 1945 Bonhoeffer gave a brief meditation for a group of prisoners being transferred to Flossenbürg concentration camp. The readings stipulated for the day were Isa 53:5 ("with his wounds we are healed") and 1 Pet 1:3 ("Blessed be the God and Father of our Lord Jesus Christ! By his great mercy we have been born anew to a living hope through the resurrection of Jesus Christ from the dead"). He was hanged early the next day.[44] Nothing survives of this meditation. The Isaiah text is quoted in 1 Pet 2:24. The seeds are present in these two texts of the counter-intuitive identity he exhibited, an identity which is founded in suffering shared with Jesus. Thus he was led into facing devastating life with hope engendered by trust in sharing the power of Jesus' resurrection.

In conclusion, three observations can be made.

First, the evidence suggests that 1 Peter played for Bonhoeffer an out-sized role in shaping a struggle to be a faithful witness, beginning with the initial engagement against the ideology of Nazism. The letter provided language and imagery for what he said in his Ascension Day sermon in 1933, and it was part of the last words he said before he died a martyr in 1945. At times of shocking disappointment, he turned to the letter for renewed fortitude. Some of his most penetrating theological thinking was born out of a creative interplay as he turned to 1 Peter in the context of his own suffering.

Moreover, 1 Peter provides a linkage between his Confirmation Instruction Plan and the *Cost of Discipleship* centering on the image of the alien, as well as a linkage between the *Cost of Discipleship* and the biblical study on temptation around suffering vicariously for the world's sake. In these critical theological breakthroughs, he typically cited only from 1 Peter.

In sum, Bonhoeffer found to be immensely helpful in understanding himself what scholars today identify as the epistle's addressees: aliens in

---

44. The incident is widely reported. For example, Godsey, *The Theology of Dietrich Bonhoeffer*. Documented by fellow prisoner Payne Best, *The Venlo Incident*, 180.

their native state by virtue of their staking all on their confession of Christ as Lord. This provided him an identity around which he could build a life of faithfulness in his conflict with Nazism.

Second, while almost a century separates the work of Bonhoeffer and Horrell, it is remarkable how they mutually illuminate each other. Bonhoeffer traces the devastating effects of a deepening realization of becoming an exile in one's own country, an exegetical position Horrell and others have established. Likewise, the strategy of coping with persecution through committing to a counter-intuitive identity with Christ, which has received recent scholarly scrutiny in 1 Peter, finds a powerful expression in the life, witness and work of Bonhoeffer.

Third, the exegesis of 1 Peter led Bonhoeffer into an understanding of the suffering Jesus as someone who welcomed his own suffering both as an alien in his own country and as the subject of God's holy judgment on his nation. To get a sense of his suffering we have but to recall his poignant question in his 1942 essay: Have there ever been people in history who in their time, like us, had so little ground under their feet, people to whom every possible alternative open to them at the time appeared equally unbearable, senseless, and contrary to life? In letters from prison, he poured out his soul to Bethge about his being attacked by *Anfechtung*.

First Peter led Bonhoeffer to grasp that by Jesus' opening up his suffering to Bonhoeffer, by Bonhoeffer annealing his suffering to Jesus', Bonhoeffer could see that his suffering was included in Jesus' redemptive purpose. That bond also gave him access to the counter-intuitive stamina rooted in the inheritance of Jesus' resurrection. This was a theological position of great moment, crafted in the throes of an existential crisis.

Establishing this perspective allows us to examine and evaluate several attempts in recent years to claim his stature and authority. We note, with concern, attempts by polarizing figures in church and culture to use Bonhoeffer to endorse their partisan positions, whether progressive or reactionary. As noted by Charles Marsh in a review of Eric Metaxas' book, *Bonhoeffer: Pastor, Martyr, Prophet, Spy* (2010), Bonhoeffer is claimed by Christians and Jews, evangelicals and non-evangelicals, liberals and conservatives who assert that we are living in a "Bonhoeffer moment."[45] Too often those who make this claim compare the political situation which angers them to the Nazi era and drape their partisan agenda with the mantle

---

45. Marsh, "Eric Mataxas's Bonhoeffer Delusions," 2. See also the review by Green, "Hijacking Bonhoeffer." I am indebted to David J. Gouwens for pointing this out to me.

of a Bonhoeffer that is more a projection of their own partisan aims.[46] That misses fundamentally the depth of his realism of our deep complicity in that which we oppose.[47] The profundity of his witness of a sober discipline of prayer, suffering and being for others must be recovered for the search for faithfulness in our Trumpian time.

46 Haynes has written of this takeover of Bonhoeffer in *The Battle for Bonhoeffer*. See in particular his comments on the "populist" Bonhoeffer employed in the 2016 victory of Donald J. Trump for the U. S. presidency, 85–112.

47. Barnett in an essay for *The Washington Post,* April 9, 2015, reminds us that "In 1936, he filled out the required political questionnaire and provided an 'Aryan certificate' in an attempt to keep his teaching position. He was brought into the resistance only as a ploy to keep him out of Hitler's army. Once there, he found himself part of a plot that included a wide range of figures, some of them honorable, others men who had fully participated in Nazi deeds before ultimately turning against the regime." "Bonhoeffer is Widely Beloved," Cited in Haynes, *The Battle for Bonhoeffer*, 132.

5

The Use of 1 Peter by Aliens in the Modern Era, Part 2

CIRCUMSTANCES OF BEING ALIEN have continued to prompt Christians in the modern era to turn to 1 Peter as a source of nurture and guidance for the contemporary church's life and witness. It is time now to move beyond Bonhoeffer and ask the question: how has 1 Peter been accessed in the light of the options laid out by Elliott, Balch, and Horrell? Has current scholarship on this first-century writing guided modern readers who are made to feel aliens in their native land towards insight and support? Do the various understandings of alien-ship or Christology produce different interpretations of the letter? What reading strategies have modern interpreters used in engaging this letter?

International Reception of 1 Peter

We have found a number of studies that take as their starting point Elliott's position that the addressees are principally persons forcibly settled by imperial migration who become Christians—effectively a double alienation. His portrayal of the circle of readers as resembling a sect has also found traction. His work has been welcomed internationally by communities under duress. We will discuss four such examples briefly, and conclude our international survey by describing one offered by John W. de Gruchy which anticipates the work of Horrell.

Elliott's position has been adopted as a model by Asian Christians who have emigrated to the United States. Russell C. Moy writes that even though the presence of Asians in this country today is due to voluntary emigration rather than forced migration, nevertheless 1 Peter speaks to the challenge of maintaining their ethnic identity within a foreign and sometimes hostile country. This challenge becomes particularly intense when conversion to Christianity brings the consequence of suffering ostracism from their family.[1] The sectarian nature of Elliott's portrayal of the readers of 1 Peter resonates with the sect-like qualities of the Chinese Christian communities in the United States and is designed to preserve ethnic identity.

Similarly, Fika J. Van Rensburg in his 1998 study of Afrikaans speaking Christians begins with Elliott's understanding of Christians as "resident and visiting aliens." He observes how many "South Africans (especially Afrikaans speaking South Africans) currently experience their position as being aliens in their own country."[2] The author assumes that the reader knows what this experience is, since he declines to describe it and thereby chooses not to validate or invalidate their experience. Given the history of apartheid,[3] this could mean that Van Rensburg sees them as native-born non-Africans. The essay argues that Afrikaans speaking South African Christians when facing discrimination should exercise their constitutional rights; and if their appeal fails, they are to follow the epistle's counsel and adopt a position of non-retaliation while continuing to do good. The sectarian character of Afrikaans speaking South African Christians seems evident, given their self-understanding as native-born non-natives facing discrimination.

Valdir R. Steuernagel offered an essay originally published in 1986 and reissued in 2016[4] in which he writes out of his pastoral work in struggle against repressive regimes in Latin America, particularly Chile and Peru. He concentrates on 1 Pet 2:9–10. Elliott's double alienation model is part of Steuernagel's exegetical framework; however, he confuses the reader because he has native born aliens in mind. The aliens who read this letter live in "a capitalist society based on profit and consumption."[5] Steuernagel imagines that if 1 Peter were to visit Latin American, we would be invited

---

1. Moy, "Resident Aliens of the Diaspora: 1 Peter and Chinese Protestants in San Francisco," 267–78 and Chen, "Accidental Pilgrims," 95–115. In this regard, see the important work by River-Rodriguez, "Toward a Diaspora Hermeneutics," 180, who divides such a reading strategy into three tasks, reading *through* diaspora, reading *from* diaspora and reading *for* diaspora.

2. Van Rensburg, "Christians as 'Resident and Visiting Aliens,'" 573.

3. Among the extensive literature, see van der Merwe, *African Perspectives*, a collection of Black and White perspectives on South Africa,

4 Steuernagel, "An Exiled Community." Pagination is from the 2016 issue.

5 Steuernagel, "An Exiled Community." 196.

to understand life as a gift of grace and become prophets by "denouncing a style of living absolutely rooted in the idea of consumption" and by joining a community that attracts public attention through a life of being the household of God. Steuernagel highlights an observation by Donald Senior, "The love and service that binds the Christians together as God's household are the most potent witness they can offer a world starved for meaning."[6] Though the community might be sectarian by nature, it nevertheless has a mandate to be a public witness, and to anticipate harsh suffering.

The fourth example from the international impact of Elliott's ground breaking work is provided by Simeon F. Kehinde who speaks out of the agony in Nigeria of "scores of religious conflicts and crises as a result of intolerance and total disregard for human rights and reprisal attacks."[7] While Kehinde in his exegetical work on 1 Pet 2:4–10 references Elliott's understanding of the letter's recipients as forced immigrants, Kehinde's audience is native-born Nigerians. Here is another example of Elliott's work being cited to support guidance to native-born populations. Kehinde emphasizes the letter's overall purpose of encouraging absolute trust in Jesus as the necessary condition to remaining strong through whatever situation believers find themselves. Christians must remain unified in order to stand firm in the face of trials and persecution. They will stay strong as they adhere to their identity as a kingdom of priests and holy nation. They cannot let their suffering make them compromise in this conviction.

Though each of these essays come out of unique and existentially fraught circumstances, they sound the common theme of the responsibility of alien Christians to maintain their distinctive witness in the face of implacable realities of prejudice and injustice. The sect is an important source of their strength. God's underlying faithfulness remains largely unaddressed in the absence of questions of theodicy. Notably, the way the letter approaches the situation of Christian wives and slaves is not of interest.

Within the international group the witness of John W. de Gruchy occupies a special place. As a white theologian in South Africa, he was thrust into the experience of being an alien in his own land because he struggled to combat apartheid. It is not surprising that Dietrich Bonhoeffer became a major influence on his thinking.[8] In his book *Theology and Ministry in*

---

6. Steuernagel, "An Exiled Community," 203, quoting Senior, *1 & 2 Peter*, 7.

7. Kehinde "Christianity Amidst Violence," 78.

8. For a discussion of the possibilities and limits of Bonhoeffer's thinking on the struggle in South Africa, see de Gruchy, "Bonhoeffer in South Africa," in Bethge,

Context and Crisis, A South African Perspective, 1986, he engages the suffering of native South Africans, well aware of the differing and imbalanced perspectives, yet wanting to stand in solidarity and in advocacy. While his reflections on suffering are nuanced and broad, he chooses to focus on oppressive suffering, that is, suffering which is experienced as domineering, calculated, deliberate, discriminatory, and unrelenting. This is suffering which crushes resistance and makes inevitable the emergence of the question of God's faithfulness and potency.

Following Bonhoeffer, de Gruchy asserts that God's faithfulness and potency can only be upheld by a God who suffers redemptively. In the development of this thesis he cites 1 Pet 4:13, "But rejoice insofar as you are sharing Christ's sufferings, so that you may also be glad and shout for joy when his glory is revealed" to anchor his exposition of our participating in the sufferings of Christ. He begins his discussion by quoting the work of Takatso Mofokeng, whose *The Crucified Among the Crossbearers*, he judges to be "the most thorough attempt to develop a black Christology in South Africa to date."[9]

> On the cross the Father, in a unique actualization of his love for man [sic] in the world of extreme opposition to him, gave his son fully and completely to do that which is sufficient in ending the center of the power of his enemies. It is therefore no wonder that Jesus, the son, screamed the scream of God-abandonment. This is the scream of those with whom he identified and for whom he suffered. They feel, above the pain inflicted by their torturers, the excruciating pain and agony of suffering in God-abandonment at the moment they would most need him, i.e. his intervention. In this, he was indeed like us in everything. But now in Jesus' case, and here lies the difference, he experiences God-abandonment doing justice, suffers injustice in total obedience to his Father![10]

Bonhoeffer, Exile and Martyr, 26–42. Bethge's cautionary response "A Confessing Church in South Africa?" is an appendix, 167–78. How valuable Bonhoeffer's witness was in the contemporary struggle of the church in East Germany made others in similar situations look to him for inspiration. Writing from the East German perspective, Ulrich Lincoln observes that Bonhoeffer "became a leading inspiration for a church that found itself in a position of minority and opposition. In a country where the state's attitude towards the church was openly hostile, where the church's capability to work in public was restricted by a hostile ideology, Bonhoeffer's writing about radical discipleship proved to be a major inspiration for many." Electronic source. Cited by Charles Marsh in his Foreword to Haynes, *The Battle for Bonhoeffer*, x.

9. De Gruchy, *Theology and Ministry*, 116.
10. De Gruchy, *Theology and Ministry*, 116.

Mofokeng clearly enunciates the counter-intuitive position of classical soteriology, that through God-abandonment of Jesus, God ended the "center of the power of his enemies." But, de Gruchy asks, how does the God who suffers God-abandonment help us in our suffering? "How does God's grief move beyond solidarity in our pain and become redemptive?" Here de Gruchy reaches out to the metaphor found in the Old Testament of God's labor pains intensifying to the point of a new reality bursting forth, "a fresh breaking forth of creative and redemptive activity." God's suffering is redemptive as it gives birth to a new order, a new creation. Redemptive suffering is manifested in the resurrection of Jesus, the God-abandoned one. Our suffering is revalued as redemptive when we suffer for the sake of the new order, as we struggle for justice as disciples of the crucified. Thus to participate in the sufferings of Christ (1 Pet 4:13) is to see our suffering as participating in the redemptive suffering of God with full confidence of its outcome secured by the resurrection of Jesus. "God's redemptive suffering in Christ becomes concrete in the world through the life and witness of the suffering community of faith and especially its prophets."[11]

Similarly to Bonhoeffer, de Gruchy anticipates Horrell's position in accessing 1 Peter as he grasps the radically new possibilities afforded to South Africans in their suffering under horrendously imbalanced power relationships as they are embraced in the crucified-resurrected Christ.

American Reception of 1 Peter

We turn now to recent American interpretations. Joel B. Green reaches out to 1 Peter from a sense of alienation as a native son in the United States attempting to live a life of holiness in an un-holy nation. His essay positions 1 Peter within the context of how American culture trivializes faith. In naming himself as an alien, Green avoids seeing himself through either of the lenses supplied by Elliott or Balch.[12] In some respects, however, he adopts exegetical positions nearer to Horrell's. For him the ability to live as a holy alien does not require separation from the world, and it certainly does not imply conformity with social expectations. Green's careful analysis and thoughtful conclusions ask for discerning appreciation.

---

11. De Gruchy, *Theology and Ministry*, 119. For more on the theology of the abandoning God, see Bailey, *The Self-Shaming God*.

12. Green, "Living as Exiles," 323–24.

Green experiences the holy person/community in America being increasingly isolated by multiple forces. He enumerates them as: modernity's pressure on the individual to subordinate personal religious views to a public faith largely devoid of religion; compartmentalization of the sacred from the secular so that the holiness found in worship practices has no application to workaday lives; and the wedge created by the Enlightenment which is driven between the scientific study of our faith and the exercise of that faith in spiritual practices. He asks, "Where shall we find a standard for holiness in a world system bereft of its moorings to any standard of holiness outside the individual's own inclinations?"[13]

First Peter, for Green, is a letter targeted to uplift and strengthen the holiness of its readers in order to protect them from defecting against powerful inclinations to conform. Green realizes that a life of holiness may bring upon it tremendous pressures to conform to "un-holiness." Speaking of that, he writes, "God's people, including ourselves, do not embrace rejection easily. We want to belong. We want to be chosen. We want status. We do not want to be strangers, aliens, people for whom 'home' is not and can never really be 'home.'"[14] First Peter has the potential of generating a counter-pressure to keep us from capitulating.

However, for 1 Peter to shape us, Green argues that we need to put ourselves into the place of the Model Reader. Quoting Umberto Eco,[15] Green defines this as someone who can "deal with texts in the act of interpreting in the same way as the author dealt with them in the act of writing.... This requires that readers read themselves into the text, so to speak tuning their ears to the bandwidth of the text." This is the "precondition for actualizing the potential of a text to engage and transform us."[16]

With the appeal to the Model Reader, problems surface. Unfortunately, Green does not describe, other in the most general terms, what is the world of the Model Reader of 1 Peter, consequently we have little to go on in mapping out the threat leveled against the Model Reader to remaining an alien. Moreover, despite our best attempt at historical reconstruction, it is methodologically suspicious to assert that a reader can imagine her- or himself being the Model Reader in order to hear a text correctly. It is theologically suspect as well, in that an historical constraint (the so-called Model Reader)

13. Green, "Living as Exiles," 312.
14. Green, "Living as Exiles," 317.
15. *The Role of the Reader*, 7–11.
16. Green, "Living as Exiles," 312.

is placed upon the self-convicting power of scripture within a reader in any age (Calvin's "inner testimony of the Holy Spirit"). Even more, it is not our prerogative, as Green would have us to think, either to yield or to withhold our assent in the presence of the convicting power of the Holy Spirit, nor can someone persuade us to choose to accept and obey scripture.

Green's reading of 1 Peter shows that we are faced with "two competing versions of the same reality, with our experience of the world portrayed as both the worst of time . . . and the best of times . . . . Peter wants his readers, us, to read our contemporary lives from within the perspective of the scriptural story of God and the life of Jesus."[17] Green's handling of this preferred perspective leans heavily on Israel's life-story of exile, albeit construed through the life, death, and resurrection of Jesus. First Peter's Model Readers, as aliens, are to see themselves inserted into the story of Israel in exile as that anticipates Jesus' life as an exile. Both Israel and the Model Reader of 1 Peter are on a journey toward holiness.

However, for all the importance Green attaches to the Old Testament narrative, he appears to work with the Old Testament from an ahistorical position. He uses the technical term of foreshadowing (seeing "in retrospect how events happen [in the past] as a consequence of things to come")[18] to describe the production of Israel's story being driven by the as-yet unseen life of Jesus. This allows him to make the claim that "Peter collapses the historical distinctives between ancient Israel and contemporary Christians in favor of theological unity."[19] There is no need, on this accounting, for a hermeneutic which values the original story of Israel while appropriating it in fresh ways for new contexts and needs. The Old Testament becomes a book of symbols for Christian proclamation.

Jesus is the key to the life of holiness to which Green aspires. He uses three metaphors to describe how Jesus is to be our key. His life is the *warrant* for his directives to us. He is the "*interpretative matrix* for understanding the pattern of God's story" with us. And he is "the *lens* through which to read our story within the story of God."[20] Each of these metaphors contains a strong aspect of functionality. That opens the door to handling Jesus objectively, and Green follows that lead by calling Jesus a model in three

---

17. Green, "Living as Exiles," 313.
18. Green, "Living as Exiles," 319.
19. Green, "Living as Exiles," 318–19.
20. Green, "Living as Exiles," 320. Emphasis is mine.

senses: exemplary, redemptive, and anticipatory. This model contains the dimensions of our holiness.

We enter upon a life of holiness as the Holy Spirit calls us into the place of holiness and forms us as a holy people according to the model of Christ.[21] "Hence, Peter insists on a conversion of our deepest allegiances, our character, and our practices—even if this involves suffering injustice precisely because we repudiate violence by refusing to 'repay evil for evil or insulting for insulting' (3:2)." He concludes. "If we are different from the world, it is not because we set out to be so, but rather because our lives rest ultimately in a God who is different and we follow in the footsteps of Jesus Christ."[22]

Our investigation has raised questions about whether the understanding of Jesus as model is up to the task of fulfilling 1 Peter's aim in bringing pastoral care to a community under threat. The model-metaphor opens easily to objectification, manipulation, and performance. That is to say, the model metaphor places the interpreter and the interpreter's world in the dominant position of shaping the model and lessens the opportunity for genuine engagement with a transformative idea resident in the text. Jesus is not an entity to be held at arm's length, to be objectively studied and carefully imitated. On the contrary, the Jesus of 1 Peter incorporates the alien and interweaves his suffering with their suffering. Out of this shared suffering emerge new-found agency and initiatives for aliens to respond to hostile actors. The principal threat is not to holiness but to the fading of the believer's trust in the faithfulness of God to support their risk of venturing upon this new identity with new-found initiatives in the midst of a world of potential harm.

Reception by Communities of Difference

We turn now to marginalized communities in North America who find themselves under threat. Black, feminist, and queer communities have subjected 1 Peter to rigorous analysis in order to understand both the roots of their oppression as well as strategies for resisting it. For these communities, the work of New Testament scholar Elisabeth Schüssler Fiorenza has been pivotal. Her feminist exegesis informs how women as well as queer and black communities grapple with the text.[23]

---

21. Green, "Living as Exiles," 321, 323.
22. Green, "Living as Exiles," 324.
23. For a brief orientation to various interpretive approaches on offer to marginalized

Schüssler Fiorenza reaches out to 1 Peter from her self-identification as an alien in the world of her Bible. She judges her Bible as elite (kyriocentric) and male-centered (anthrocentric). This makes all women aliens with their Bible who are forced to "struggle for survival and justice on the bottom pyramid of domination and subordination, oppression and exploitation."[24] As a New Testament scholar, she reads 1 Peter in the name of women and LGBTQIA+ people who see the American Christian Right working to diminish their citizen rights. The Christian Right invokes the Bible to support the central cornerstone of its political rhetoric "because it teaches the divinely ordained subordination of wo/men and the creational differences between the sexes as well as the abomination of homosexuality."[25] Thus, her alien-making Bible also makes her an alien in her own land.

From this set of presuppositions, she criticizes much of the work of scholars who form the base of our investigation: Balch for emphasizing the letter's counsel of adaptation and conformity; Elliott for continuing to use the pattern of dominant imperial household to style his sectarian strategy; Carter for capitulating to the reality of the little power wielded by the recipients; Horrell for emptying the designation *Christianos* of all messianic connotations and solidifying a supersessionist reading of the Old Testament; and Bechtler for continuing to use the categories of honor and shame that are central to the world of elite, propertied males.[26]

Though her survey of scholars does not include the important work of Holloway, who identified 1 Peter as part of the genre of letters of consolation, she criticizes therapeutic readings of 1 Peter as coded in culturally feminist terms. By that she means someone who reads the letter as a patient "for their own private use, enjoyment and edification." This approach does not lead to "a critical liberating experience."[27] In this light any consoling would be a form of male domination.

Schüssler Fiorenza sets out to read 1 Peter for the liberation of native-born aliens, despite the fact that she judges it as a "communication sent from the imperial center . . . as an authoritative letter of advice and admonition to

---

readers, see Dinkler, "The Bible and Women?" 6–7. She describes three options: (i) extract and apply, (ii) contextualize, and (iii) reject these texts.

24. Fiorenza, *1 Peter, Reading Against the Grain*, 9.
25. Fiorenza, *1 Peter, Reading Against the Grain*, 68.
26. Fiorenza, *1 Peter, Reading Against the Grain*, 8, 30.
27. Fiorenza, *1 Peter, Reading Against the Grain*, 14.

good conduct and subordination to the colonial public of the provinces."[28] She holds that its "author represents the interests of the owner and patron class who felt prerogatives were being undermined."[29] The only way she can appropriate the letter for the purpose of liberation is to use a feminist lens of reading, a hermeneutics of reading against the grain that challenges the "blueprints of andro-kyriocentric design" embedded in the letter.[30]

As an example of her reading, two far-reaching results come out of her interpretation of 1 Pet 2:11—3:12. First, the Christological model of suffering at the heart of the letter has to be rejected, and second, the epistle's figure of Sarah as exemplary must be repudiated. She argues that the epistle uses these major figures to fund its counsel of subordination in the situations of political order and domestic order.

She notices the author's use of the rhetoric of the "winning of good will" (the *captatio benevolentiae*) in first section of the letter. By a hermeneutics of suspicion, she fingers the author's deliberate use of this rhetorical device

> to secure the sympathy or support of the recipients for doing what the author(s) tell(s) them to. Because you have been given the titles of the people of Israel [1 Pet 2:9–10], you should now behave like Christ who suffered innocently. As G*d's people who live in the midst of Gentles, they should "do good" rather than commit acts against the dominant cultural and political ethos.[31]

The author links claiming Israel's honorific titles with following the example of Christ.

Schüssler Fiorenza breaks this linkage, dispensing with Christology. By reading against the grain, Schüssler Fiorenza turns the text against itself by imagining how those who are made subservient might have spoken had they not been snubbed. Rather than using the call to follow in the steps of the suffering Christ to provide a warrant for directing Christian slaves to submit to harsh masters, a counter-reading would key off of the appellations "you are a royal priesthood and a chosen race" which slaves would use to demand that the Christian community collect enough money to purchase their freedom. In a similar move, rather than using the example of Sarah to stiffen the backbone of Christian wives to submit to unbelieving husbands, a counter-reading would start from the commission of "proclaiming the

---

28. Fiorenza, *1 Peter, Reading Against the Grain*, 23.
29. Fiorenza, *1 Peter, Reading Against the Grain*, 59.
30. Fiorenza, *1 Peter, Reading Against the Grain*, 10.
31. Fiorenza, *1 Peter, Reading Against the Grain*, 56.

great deeds of the one who had called them out of darkness into his marvelous light" to direct these women to divorce their husbands that they might be free to pursue their commission.[32]

Behind this reading there must stand a radically different picture of Jesus. He is not the center of a counter-intuitive identity which is bound up in the mystery of his victory in suffering, nor is it a source of new agency. Rather, he is the leader of Messianist Jews whose understanding of being the covenant people of God is "hugely democratic in practice.... *Christianoi* are Messianist Jews who are seen as seditious and as a threat to colonial religious, cultural and political Roman imperial 'customs.'"[33]

Schüssler Fiorenza argues that people who are aliens in their own country can construct a counter identity against one rooted in subordination by deconstructing and re-imagining the vision of 1 Peter. Jettisoning traditional Christology as inculcating subordination and re-presenting Jesus as a leader of a democratic community, she adopts the socio-cultural criterion that "The output of exegesis must first be accountable to the victims."[34] Reading against the grain, she points her search for visions of wellbeing in the direction of biblical texts such as 1 Peter and makes them proclaim the divine as a power for justice and wellbeing. In this process, she is convinced that the community will gain power and stamina to struggle for a society free from structures of domination.

A striking example of a North American community under threat using the work of Schüssler Fiorenza to access 1 Peter is supplied by Robin Gorsline's entry on the epistle in *The Queer Bible Commentary*.[35] His indebtedness to Elliott is clear: "Queer people," he writes, "can identify with the 'resident aliens' and 'strangers' of 1 Peter, . . . living, as we do, among those who, at best, so often do not understand us and, at worst, actively revile us. . . . We who adhere to different sexual practices can seem to be threats to the natural order in which they so fervently believe."[36]

Gorsline admits real concerns that the letter does not fit well into contemporary queer life. The difference in the character of the opposition between 1 Peter's audience and today's queers presents the first challenge to how queers can make use of this letter. Whereas the conflict in 1 Peter

---

32. Fiorenza, *1 Peter, Reading Against the Grain*, 74.
33. Fiorenza, *1 Peter, Reading Against the Grain*, 56.
34. Fiorenza, *1 Peter, Reading Against the Grain*, 76.
35. Gorsline, "1 Peter," 724–32.
36. Gorsline, "1 Peter," 742.

was between Christians' religious beliefs and practices in the face of the dominant non-Christian culture, for queers it is their sexual lives that upset social arrangements that their opponents (including some in the church!) believe provide the foundations of social order.

The second challenge is that "the strategies [of the writer of 1 Peter] in response to this opposite . . . hold questionable appeal to queers today. For example, 1 Peter resorts to strategies that rely on achieving some level of acceptance by those who are most critical of the communities in question."[37]

Both of these challenges stem from the Gorsline's position of making human experience the dominant filter for judging the usefulness of a text's interpretation. Gorsline asks, "Can Christian, or other, queers draw upon [this book] in the Christian scriptures for a word of hope in a hostile world?[38] His answer is conditioned on adopting several exegetical decisions.

Chief among those decisions is to reject any proposal that results in reading the message of the letter as capitulation to dominating powers. Both solutions of Elliott and Balche fail as they underscore the letter's admonitions to behave in socially acceptable ways. He references Schüssler Fiorinza's scheme which identifies the instigators of conflict as uppity slaves and feisty wives who claim equality in the name of Christ. This rings truer to earning the acceptance by queers of the letter's authority.

Following hard on this initial decision on what is a valid interpretation, is the attempt to describe the intra-community power dynamics behind the text. Gorsline argues that the slaves and wives so admonished "represent the true spirit of a religious consciousness that is being tamped down in this letter, albeit in response to apparent pressure from the larger culture."[39] This is to say, using a hermeneutics of suspicion, Gorsline holds that the author of the letter cynically took advantage of the conflict between Christians' beliefs/practices and the dominant non-Christian culture as an opportunity to squash an intra-church fight between patriarchal pastoral leadership and the community's new upstarts.

This scenario links with a radically revised view of Jesus. Gorsline follows Schüssler Fiorinza and Corley in rejecting the letter's "deep identification in suffering with the suffering of Jesus. This spiritualizing of the faith has social consequences in history, slavery and violence against women."[40] The

37. Gorsline, "1 Peter," 744.
38. Gorsline, "1 Peter," 725.
39. Gorsline, "1 Peter," 728.
40. Gorsline, "1 Peter,"

author "relies too much on a suffering servant concept of atonement which perpetuates cycles of violence and victimization and holds up the victims as a model for women.... 'Christian suffering' should become a vehicle for social change, not a means of social assimilation as in 1 Peter."[41]

Indeed, for Corley, who is a major influence on Gorsline, the message in 1 Peter of suffering like Christ is extremely problematic and renders, finally, the letter unusable as Christian scripture.[42] She sees the letter portraying the suffering Jesus as the example of noble behavior that is to be followed by people in submission because they will be rewarded when Christ returns. She evaluates the example of Jesus' non-retaliation as a directive for a submissive response to oppression, which the letter's author hopes will stoke pity and wonder from hostile observers and deflect attention away from the larger Christian community.

This directive for behavior, Corley argues is supported by the letter's theory of atonement, which posits "God as an abusive patriarch who demands the punishment of his Son in order to satisfy his wrath and honor. ... For feminists, such imitation merely perpetuates a cycle of victimization, violence, and abuse.... As in reality victimization does not lead to vindication, feminists argue that such an image not only trivializes human suffering but encourages passivity in Christians, particularly women."[43]

Instead of a Christology with a suffering Jesus at its heart, Gorsline reads against the grain and advocates a "Jesus who never shied away from conflict. He almost seems to seek it out and encourage it. That difference—on the one hand, seeking to avoid conflict, and on the other, seeking it out or at least not avoiding conflict—is the key to understanding this text, and also to understanding how we, as queers, today can relate to it."[44]

"Can this book be saved?" asks Gorsline. His answer is, "the practical effect—when you are among the oppressed—is to view this text as a call to avoid further difficulty with the powers-that-are." Its author is a leader who does not want to "rock the boat." Therefore, "Queers cannot take the text as a sourcebook for strategy and tactics to achieve liberation." Reading against the grain, he encourages not to identify with the author, but with the boat-rockers the author addresses.[45]

---

41. Gorsline, "1 Peter," 729, quoting Corley, "1 Peter," 355.
42. Corley, "1 Peter," 354–55.
43. Corley, "1 Peter," 354.
44. Gorsline, "1 Peter," 731.
45. Gorsline, "1 Peter," 732.

A similar counter-reading is proposed by Larry George in his entry on 1 Peter in an African-American commentary, *True to our Native Land*.[46] George recognizes that the unspeakably tragic circumstances of slavery and its legacy make it immediately apparent to Black readers that they are modern day versions of pilgrims and aliens. Theirs is a double burden of alien-ship. On the one hand, they were brought forcibly to this country and resettled in extremely perilous circumstances as chattel, a situation which Elliott's model recognizes. On the other hand, some became aliens in their own, new country by conversion to Christianity. This is a view of being alien that is advanced by Horrell. George explains,

> Indeed, several people of the African diaspora can readily identify with the theme of suffering associated with baptism because they too sought baptism or conversion to Christianity as a way to subvert their status as chattel slaves and sought to become full citizens because of their newly found Christian faith. Instead, their chattel status remained the same, and some were forbidden this rite of baptism by their slave masters. Not only did the newly converted slaves find hostility from slave masters, but also other slaves thought that such a move was an act of treason because these converted slaves abandoned their former gods.[47]

George is well aware of how the oppressive official text of 1 Peter has been used to solidify subservient behavior to those with superior power, particularly as this affects how women and people of color have been dominated by (white) men. This is a reading which must be combatted by a "hermeneutics of suspension" that results in a "resistant inclusive liberating reading."[48] Read this way, 1 Peter is a type of resistant literature for use in situations of implacable oppression that cannot be directly overthrown. However, the tactic of non-violent resistance, which George's exegesis brings out, is not tied tightly to being bound to Jesus but rather is rooted in some general theory of liberation. In fact, George heavily criticizes the oppressive counsel to subservient people to accept suffering "as Christ did in order to find God's favor."[49] Instead, George thinks that 1 Peter advocates for oppressed people to live as freed people (even though they are not) so that their behavior "will require non-Christians or foolish people to treat

46. George, "1 Peter," 476–87.
47. George, "1 Peter," 478.
48. George, "1 Peter," 481.
49. George, "1 Peter," 483.

them as freed persons."⁵⁰ Thus Christians do not have counter-intuitive identities bound up in Jesus. Instead, they have counterfeit identities designed to trick people as a strategy for survival.

As Jesus is not the source for counter-intuitive living, George gives him the role of providing the motivation for never giving up, no matter how miniscule the resistance. The hope of eventual liberation is anchored in the "futuristic, eschatological . . . parousia of Jesus Christ." He explains, "in order to survive in the present, one must have a *telos*, a goal much bigger than one can realize alone. This hope is central . . . because it is through hope that the reader is mentally and spiritually strengthened. There is also a past foundation for this hope, namely, Jesus Christ's death and resurrection, which resulted in his glory."⁵¹

While there are many points of difference among the interpreters we have discussed, it is yet possible to organize them into servicing one of two large categories of orientation: communities organized to confront the oppressive social order and communities organized to preserve self-identity (sect).

Guided by Horrell's position that the addressees are largely native-born who now turn on the Empire, examples of modern interpreters who help communities confront oppressive social orders are: Bonhoeffer, de Gruchy, Mofokeng, and Steuernagel. The scholars who write out of communities suffering from structural sexism, racism and homophobia (Schüssler Fiorenza, George, and Gosline/Cosby) also confront oppressive social orders. However, the epistle's example of a suffering Jesus coupled with advice to slaves and wives which to them is repressive proves too much to follow. This causes these scholars to break the link between the Christology of the letter and the wellspring for new agency in the face of an implacable social order.

Guided by Elliott's position that the addressees need to concentrate on preserving their uniqueness in sect-like structures, we note how this model lays the groundwork for Moy, Van Rensburg, Kehinde, Green, Liebengood, and Holloway. These scholars commonly emphasize the role of human performance measured against an ideal example of Jesus.

---

50. George, "1 Peter," 482.
51. George, "1 Peter," 480.

THE USE OF 1 PETER BY ALIENS IN THE MODERN ERA, PART 2

Hauerwas and Willimon's *Resident Aliens*

Among contemporary scholars and parish theologians who have thought deeply about Christian identity as being of an alien nature, the work of Stanley Hauerwas and William Willimon has been widely influential. Their book *Resident Aliens, Life in the Christian Colony* makes the claim: "The church is a colony, an island of one culture in the middle of another. In baptism our citizenship is transferred from one dominion to another, and we become, in whatever culture we find ourselves, resident aliens."[52]

We share similar themes, such as the totalitarian nature of empire, the countercultural nature of the Christian life and the powerful work of worship in shaping a distinctive identity. However, we describe what it means to be a resident alien from different perspectives, and we differ on basic strategies of relating to the world in which we find ourselves as aliens.

Hauerwas and Willimon use as their source text Phil 2:5–11; 3:20–21. There the Christian community is described as a πολίτευμα "commonwealth" which they construe, following Moffatt's translation "We are a colony of heaven." They further explain: "A colony is a beachhead, an outpost, an island of one culture in the middle of another, a place where the values of home are reiterated and passed on to the young, a place where the distinctive language and life-style of the resident aliens are lovingly nurtured and reinforced."[53]

The Jewish Diaspora model fills in the contours of life in this colony:

> The Jews in Dispersion were well acquainted with what it meant to live as strangers in a strange land, aliens trying to stake out a living on someone else's turf. Jewish Christians had already learned, in their day-to-day life in the synagogue how important it was for resident aliens to gather to name the name, to tell the story, to sing Zion's songs in a land that didn't know Zion's God.[54]

Our investigation differs in that we seek to understand Christian identity as lived by the addresses of 1 Peter. We hold that they are Gentile persons, principally, who have suddenly made themselves aliens in their own land by reason of their confessing Christ as Lord and becoming members

---

52. Hauerwas, *Risident Aliens*, 11.
53. Hauerwas, *Risident Aliens*, 11.
54. Hauerwas, *Risident Aliens*, 11–12.

of the Christian community. Using conventional language for proselytes, they call themselves strangers and sojourners.[55]

A second point of difference shows up in the strategies Christian aliens are to use for engaging the dominant culture. Hauerwas and Willimon seek to turn the church away from linking with any form of the dominant political or economic structure. This, to them, is a strategy of accommodation to worldly power which brings with it the demise of the church. "Both conservative and liberal church, the so-called private and public church, are basically accommodationist . . . in their social ethic. Both assume wrongly that the American church's primary social task is to underwrite American democracy."[56] Rather than being acolytes for American democracy, the church is to learn "how to be faithful to a strange community, which is shaped by a story of how God is with us."[57]

In contrast, our investigation must take account of 1 Peter's advice to "Honor everyone. Love the family of believers. Fear God. Honor the emperor" (2:17). As we have shown in the example of Dietrich Bonhoeffer, this is a more arduous discipleship than what Hauerwas and Willimon have in mind. For them, it is sufficient to attend to life within the colony which they detail as "a place clearly visible to the world where people are faithful to their promises, love their enemies, tell the truth, honor the poor, suffer for righteousness, and thereby testify to the amazing community-creating power of God."[58] Whether this makes an impact on the world is of secondary nature. Faithfulness, they say, trumps effectiveness.

Bonhoeffer, on the contrary, makes the radical claim that to fear God and honor the emperor finally requires one to place oneself under the judgment of the empire, and in that submission to the judgment of the empire to bear God's judgment of the empire. Thus the gathering of aliens serves the empire by vicariously, with Christ, bearing the judgment of the empire for them. This acceptance of redemptive suffering can only be sustained by employing a conscious understanding of being engrafted into Christ who bears God's judgment of the world on the cross. By being so engrafted, one is put in contact with Christ's resurrection stamina. As we live out of resurrection stamina, we will follow Jesus as a human for others.

55. Horrell, "'Race', 'Nation', 'People,'" 156 cites Sechrest, *A Former Jew*, 97–105, who explores the concept that *paroikos* and *parepidaamos* are proselyte terminology.
56. Hauerwas, *Risident Aliens*, 32.
57. Hauerwas, *Risident Aliens*, 30.
58. Hauerwas, *Risident Aliens*, 46.

Finally, there is a major distinction between us on the nature of the opposition to God's aliens brought by the dominant culture. Hauerwas and Willimon formulate American democracy as a system designed to cater to the individual and individual rights, desires and freedoms.[59] This is the system against which the community-directed life experiences of the colony sets itself. "The church rejects the world with few exceptions."[60] But they do not address the reality that it is the world of democratic liberalism which gives to the colony of heaven a freedom to exist as an outlier. In fact, the world as it is shows that it could care less about the colony until it sees that the colony could work toward its advantage. While saying that the church must be ready for hostility to its truth, they do not inquire into what could trigger that persecution.

This book argues that 1 Peter supplies a picture of opposition and threat to the gathering of aliens. It takes the form of the empire with its totalizing dynamic, which tolerates no exception to demonstrating absolute submission to the autocratic dominance of life. This is what the community that confesses Christ as Lord must distinguish itself from. This is what the community that confesses Christ as Lord must interact with. The cross is the sign of what happens to aliens when Caesar sees that the church is taking God's account of reality more seriously than Caesar's. First Peter comforts these aliens by reminding them how they have been embraced by the faithfulness of God shown to Jesus in bringing him to eschatological life out of abandonment and shame. It is to this hope that they cling for their own stamina, verve and work.

In the following chapter we will engage in a critical appraisal of the use of 1 Peter by communities under threat and draw conclusions for interpreters who find themselves faced with new forms of alien-ship.

---

59. Hauerwas, *Risident Aliens*, 32.
60. Hauerwas, *Risident Aliens*, 47.

6

Conclusions

IN THIS BOOK WE have sought to enlarge upon the position staked out by David Horrell and others that those who heard 1 Peter were, largely, persons who were native-born in first-century Anatolia. They became "sojourners and pilgrims" by virtue of their being persuaded to renounce religious practices that were the spiritual basis of state and society and to confess Christ as Lord.

Their alien status stemmed from this confession which put them at odds with normative religious, cultural, and political expectations in the Roman Empire. By refusing to take part in religious ceremonies venerating Caesar as god, their patriotic loyalty came under suspicion. This rendered them vulnerable to prosecutorial punishment. The loyalty demanded by the implacable dominance of empire was threatened by their new loyalty to Christ. Some suffered in fiery trials as Christians.

Our reading of the epistle noticed that the author paired statements of God's faithfulness with encouragements to readers to remain faithful under pressure. The direction of this dynamic connection suggests that the author of the letter wants to put forward the claim that readers can count on God's faithfulness undergirding their stamina against recanting. The presence of this pairing throughout the epistle indicates the importance the author gave to this claim and provokes the question of whether in the minds of converts the credibility of God's presence in the community was being threatened by their experience of fiery trials.

This dynamic coordination between God's credibility and human capability is fueled by several authorial decisions. First, the author structures the letter after the form of the classical letter of consolation which was commonly used to address situations of hardship. The conventional purpose of such letters of consolation was to dilute the shock of the upsetting event and to facilitate a quick recovery. However, the author moves the point of 1 Peter away from lessening the shock of the fiery trial to focusing believers on being embraced in the life and destiny of Christ. The author draws upon a mature Christology which presents Jesus as God's Son who was abandoned and put to shame on the cross and vindicated with honor in his resurrection. By being incorporated into him, believers know that their suffering is melded into his suffering, so that his power is now available to them in the midst of their suffering. This becomes the foundation of believers' new, counter-intuitive identity which gives them access to new behaviors with which to confront persecution.

Second, the author funds this new, counter-intuitive identity from the story of Israel. The copious appearance of texts from the Old Testament has drawn considerable scholarly attention, but what has not been sufficiently studied is the particular use the author makes of textual material from the Book of the Twelve. Our book provides an insight into how the author accessed the Twelve in two broad ways. First, the Twelve supplied texts that contribute to the author's telling of the story of Israel. Second, because we know from Sirach and Qumran that the Twelve was already at that time valued as a book of comfort for Jews living in diaspora, we make the case that its canonically shaped message of counter-intuitive living has contributed to shaping the mind of the author. In Israel's development of its counter-intuitive life, Israel had already taken up this strategy for remaining the people of God which now God has reaffirmed in the life and destiny of Jesus.

The modern world presents clear instances of Christians living as aliens in their own country. While circumstances will vary widely, Christian alien-ship is a current, world-wide experience. The factor necessary to cause this situation is the presence of a superior, malevolent force set in implacable opposition against Christian identity. Against such opposition, questions of both human capability to maintain Christian identity and of divine credibility to uphold this identity can run rampant. In such situations persecuted people turn to 1 Peter.[1]

---

1. It is important for interpreters to be guided by the particular circumstances surrounding the letter's production, for its message is targeted to people living under severe constraint. As George, "1 Peter," 482, notes regarding the letter's advice to women and slaves, "This code, however, was not intended to be relevant for all times, only those times when persecution and trials would necessitate resistance to avoid persecution as wrongdoers." George recognizes correctly the unique place of the letter in the canon, even though this recognition has the effect of neutralizing for contemporary use what is said to marginalized populations.

In the previous two chapters we presented a sampling of how 1 Peter has been accessed over the last eighty years. One must be careful when drawing far-reaching conclusions from such a small group of different examples. However, in this concluding chapter, we will venture some observations.

It is astonishing how communities all over the world, whether native born or immigrant, have found so accessible in 1 Peter the nurture they need to survive under a wide variety of "fiery trials." Many authors write with passion about the suffering of their reading communities, and they draw from 1 Peter the resources to minister to their audiences. The nature of the presence of a superior, malevolent force set in implacable opposition against Christian identity varies widely. Sometimes it is a clearly drawn confrontation, exampled by Bonhoeffer's struggle with Nazism, de Gruchy's with South African apartheid, Steuernagle's with South American neo-liberalism, Kehinle's with Nigerian tribalism, and the struggles of feminist (Schüssler Fiorenza), queer (Gorsline and Corley), and black (George) exegetes. Other times, the opposition is more subtle as in Green's coming to terms with a culture devoid of holiness.

Even so, we are also struck by the awkward application by some authors of Elliott's model of double-alienation as a tool to understand the particular crises of their reading communities. His model does not provide the best analogy. Unfortunately, many authors were not able to be informed by Horrell's work. Would they have been able to understand their situation in a better light if they had been able to understand the original readers as native-born aliens? We note that among those exegetes we examined, only the theological exegesis of Bonhoeffer and de Gruchy has anticipated him.

As we look at the non-North American writers we have cited, the intensity of how they experienced their threat is sharp. Steuernagel suffered the repressive regimes of Peru and Chile; Kehinde wrote out of the agony of religious conflict in Nigeria. De Gruchy labored in solidarity with black South Africans suffering under the crushing repression of the apartheid regime. He was burdened not only by the ostracism from fellow white South African opponents but also by the sense of guilt in being part of a society of the oppressors.

It is significant that the interpreters who worked out of situations of severe persecution founded their public theology on the letter's mature Christology. Those under the most stress found in 1 Peter a Jesus who was an open and accessible figure to whom a suffering one could anneal themselves to find a source for inner strength. This is the only basis from which they could implore their readers not to deviate from counter-intuitive behaviors and not to capitulate, no matter the cost. Only by readers positioning themselves within a suffering Jesus can this letter be useful as a source of comfort.

We compared these interpreters with those who study 1 Peter from a position of marginalization within the relative physical safety of the United States. Contrasts immediately show up. The letter's Christological position described in earlier chapters and which operated to varying degrees with non-North American examples, is either ignored or deliberately rejected. Consequently, the letter's understanding of what it means to live counter-intuitively as a believer in Christ is not exploited to its full pastoral ramifications for dealing with oppressive structures. The emphasis is on Jesus as the objective model against which believers are to align their behavior.[2] These contrasts will be more fully explored.

Schüssler Fiorenza faults Warren and Horrell for their practice of reading strategies for survival out of the counsel of 1 Peter. To her this is another instance of kyriocentric interpretation designed to ensure subordination of women and slaves. Yet, she can be faulted for not showing a full recognition of the realties encompassing slavery in the Roman Empire, and the *constricted options available* to subordinated persons.[3] Her suggestions for counter-readings for slaves and wives seem rather foolhardy in the context of those harsh realities.

Furthermore, in her single-minded commitment to the rule that any legitimate exegetical results must pass muster before the oppressed, she rejects its emphasis on the example of Jesus' suffering because this example further victimizes subordinate persons. Consequently, she overthrows the Christology of a suffering Jesus, at the heart of the letter, which opens itself straight on to the damages of the suffering of the oppressed. Her feminist critique of the letter renders God as a patriarchal despot demanding satisfaction on the cross for hurt honor. However, this position is flatly contradicted by the letter's insistence that the cross is God's action to put oppression to death in the death of the Son, requiring the Son to commit in utter trust to the will of God, who vindicates that trust in the resurrection (1 Pet 2:23–25). As a consequence, she deprives herself and her readers of a truly transformative message.

2. Green nominates the Holy Spirit as the agent of formation which brings the believer into the field of holiness and enables the believer to align behavior with that of Jesus.

3. For an extensive accounting of the complexity of the master-slave relationship, see Martin, *Slavery as Salvation*.

Our contention is that a new-found agency is given to the oppressed whose sufferings become sealed onto the suffering body of Christ wherein they find new and unexpected strength for counter-intuitive action even in their subordinate status. We point to the examples of Bonhoeffer, de Gruchy, and Mofokeng. They saw that by linking their suffering, under the crushing blows of Nazism and apartheid, to Christ's, a way opened up for them to preserve meaning and agency in a situation of rapidly diminishing options. These theologian-pastors did not see 1 Peter as a problematic book, to be corrected by a hermeneutics of suspicion, suspension, or subversion. For those who must live faithfully under implacable circumstances, following a suffering Jesus is the only avenue toward stamina and hope.

We maintain this is precisely what the author of 1 Peter is claiming when the two test cases of believing slaves of unbelieving masters and believing wives of unbelieving husbands ("suffering slaves and terrified wires")[4] are addressed. It is well to recall the observation of Miroslav Volf: "[1 Pet 3:9] speaks of sovereign serenity and sets a profound revaluation in motion. When blessing replaces rage and revenge, the one who suffers violence refuses to retaliate in kind and chooses instead to encounter violence with an embrace. . . . Only those who refuse to be defined by their enemies can bless them."[5] The consequence of this freedom is that the believer opens up the possibility of even the opponent coming to perceive a different way of life.

We affirm that 1 Peter has been grossly misused to further cement marginalized persons—women, blacks, LGBTQIA+ persons—in the depths of degradation. These interpretations must be vigorously confronted and debunked. We vigorously affirm that marginalized persons are made to suffer as aliens in their own land. Even so, part of the responsibility of the interpreter is to celebrate the emergence of new, Christologically based initiatives within the constraints of the historical moment. It is the interpreter's responsibility to pursue the implications of that initiative within the contemporary moment with its unique possibilities and constraints.

Finally, making 1 Peter function as a manifesto for liberation breaks the integrity of the letter. This break creates an opening to rush in with assorted ideologies. By naming the divine as a power for justice and well-being, Schüssler Fiorenza re-opens the problems of divine faithfulness and human capability in the face of implacable power imbalances that refuse

---

4. Corley, "1 Peter," 352.
5. Volf, "Soft Difference," 21–22.

CONCLUSIONS

to yield to the call for justice and well-being. The only workable answer to this stone-walling is trusting utterly that one's sufferings are embraced by a suffering Christ and launching out on the gamble that the suffering one lives and acts within the field of Christ's resurrection hope.

In his exegesis as an African American, George elevated the role eschatology plays in providing the motivation for never giving up, no matter how miniscule the resistance. The hope of eventual liberation is anchored in the "futuristic, eschatological . . . parousia of Jesus Christ. . . . [I[t is only through hope that the reader is mentally and spiritually strengthened. There is also a past foundation for this hope, namely, Jesus Christ's death and resurrection, which resulted in his glory."[6] Though George does not use Jesus' death and resurrection as the immersion point for supporting the believer in extreme stress, his comment points up the crucial role an eschatological qualifier plays in 1 Peter.

It is important to remember that 1 Peter opens with what can be called an eschatological qualifier:

> Blessed be the God and Father of our Lord Jesus Christ! By his great mercy he has given us a new birth into a living hope through the resurrection of Jesus Christ from the dead, and into an inheritance that is imperishable, undefiled, and unfading, kept in heaven for you, who are being protected by the power of God through faith for a salvation ready to be revealed in the last time. (1:3–5)

Early on in this study we pointed to how 1 Pet 4:12–19 conveyed the assurance that a counter-intuitive identity already holds within it eschatological blessings. By virtue of being born anew, the believer is placed within the eschatological field of force. This field of force qualifies the harsh exigencies of the believer's life. During the course of this investigation we have seen how this qualifier exerts certain powers on one who is bound to Christ and finds himself or herself an alien in the midst of implacable and unmovable power imbalances. This qualifier has these dimensions:

An eschatological qualifier is generated as the result of being so overwhelmed by the demonstration of God's faithfulness in the resurrection of the crucified Son that one risks his or her life in all its precariousness to that future as well.

An eschatological qualifier on suffering does not excuse the suffering as a necessary test of faithfulness nor does it participate in the enabling of victimization by being silent on structures of domination-submission.

6. George, "1 Peter," 480.

An eschatological qualifier re-sets the conditions under which suffering is endured. It blocks the ultimate intention of the imposition of suffering which is dehumanization and apostasy.

An eschatological qualifier changes or alters the experience of suffering by placing upon it the possibility of being aligned with God's suffering for the ultimate goodness of humanity, and by giving the suffering one new responses to those causing the suffering which preserve agency and dignity in situations calculated to grind a person down.

An eschatological qualifier infuses the richness of God's joy into the struggles of the believer's engagement with harsh reality which give the believer a steady source of stamina and verve.

What might this imply for an American interpreter who senses keenly what it means to be an alien in one's own land? As I write these words, the United States House of Representatives and Senate have completed the process of impeaching and trying President Donald J. Trump, which resulted in his acquittal. This tortuous event will continue to tear at the fabric of being a citizen of a "United States of America." Regardless of this outcome, the mindset that grips large swaths of Americans will not change. I do not refer to the polarized perceptions and positions advocated by "red" or "blue" citizens. No, something more basic and common to both camps will continue powerfully to inform their respective ideologies and behaviors.

That basic factor is the shared assumption of decline.[7] Both older evangelicals and younger millennials, both conservatives and progressives, are operating out of a mindset that assumes that things will continue to go downhill for them regardless of efforts to change course.

In an essay for *The Washington Post* Elizabeth Bruenig shares extensive reporting with white fundamentalist evangelical Christians in the Dallas-Fort Worth metroplex who steadfastly support the President.[8] She began

---

7. I am indebted to David Brooks for this insight. See his "Impeach Trump. And Then Move On."

8. I am well aware of voters who do not identify themselves as fundamentalist evangelicals who support President Trump's election. I am also aware that not all who call themselves evangelicals support the President. See Worthen, "What Would Jesus Do About Inequality?" For an insightful probe into the struggle within the evangelical movement over how to respond to the movement supporting white supremacy, see Worthen, "Can Black Evangelicals Save the Whole Movement?" The editorial written by Mark Galli "Trump Should Be Removed from Office," which appeared in the December 19, 2019, issue of the evangelical magazine *Christianity Today*, is further evidence that the evangelical movement is not monolithic. The vociferous opposition by the President to this editorial, who was joined by a broad array of evangelical leaders, has led observers

her essay "In God's Country" with an interview with Robert Jeffress, an influential evangelical pastor of First Baptist Church in Dallas, Texas, who is closely aligned with President Trump. She asked him: Why evangelicals have continued to support such a worldly man? Jeffress responded,

> As a Christian, I believe that regardless of what happens in Washington, DC, that the general trajectory of evangelicalism is going to be downward until Christ returns. . . . I think most Christians I know see the election of Donald Trump as maybe a respite, a pause in that [trajectory]. Perhaps to give Christians the ability and freedom more to share the gospel of Christ with people before the ultimate end occurs and the Lord returns.[9]

This explanation was surprising to Bruenig, leading her to observe, "Rather than renewing a culture in peril . . . Jeffress seemed to view Trump as someone who might carve out a temporary provisional space for evangelicals to manage their affairs."[10] Jeffress used the word "accommodation" to refer to what Trump has done to protect evangelicals from having to participate in the degradation of culture created by pro-choice, gay-friendly, immigrant-welcoming, and feminist Americans. She elaborates that "Jeffress is hardly alone in believing that evangelicals need some sort of special accommodations from a society that doesn't share their values and that they feel persecuted by." She cites a Pew Research Center survey that shows "roughly 50 percent of Americans believe evangelicals face some or a lot of discrimination." She concludes: "it makes sense that a figure such as Trump should inherit its [evangelicals'] dimming twilight and all the anger, despair, and darkness that dashed dreams entail."[11]

Bruenig discovered through speaking with a cross-section of fundamentalist evangelicals in the Dallas-Fort Worth metroplex that Jeffress' views were widely shared. As one woman from rural Farmersville told her, "What space are we going to have to be able to live in and follow our beliefs . . . without a president willing to carve out such provisions [such as his Supreme Court nominations] despite widespread criticism?" Thus Bruenig

---

to comment on how Trump's signature style combining animosity with mockery has shaped the evangelical movement in his own mold, much as he has done with the Republican Party. See Dias and Peters, "Evangelical Leaders Close Ranks." It is estimated that one third of those who voted for Trump are white evangelicals.

9 Bruenig, "In God's Country," 15–16.

10. Bruenig, "In God's Country," 17. For a collection of encomiums heralding Trump as chosen by God, see Haynes, *The Battle for Bonhoeffer*, 144–45.

11. Bruenig, "In God's Country," 19.

was confronted with the paradox that "Trump, is able, by being less Christian than your average Christian, to protect Christians who fear incursions from a hostile dominant culture."[12]

Bruenig's field reporting is complemented by an earlier in-depth study by Arlie Russell Hochschild whose book *Strangers in Their Own Land* documents the lived experience of a group of staunchly conservative residents of southwest Louisiana who sense that their "way of life" is being choked off by a circle of threats, ranging from environmental disaster to being looked down upon by liberal elites. The typical religious response to this threat is to reach for the default position of waiting out their plight until the Lord returns in the Second Coming. The place of the church is to reinforce an individual's "*moral strength to endure* [more] than on the will to change the circumstances that called on that strength. [Worship] offered a collective, supportive arena . . . within which it was safe to feel helpless, sad, or lost."[13]

The deep feeling of being on a downward glide path until the rapture comes is truly widespread. Hochschild cites a 2010 Pew Research Center report that "41 percent of all Americans believe the Second Coming 'probably' or 'definitely' will happen by the year 2050."[14] In addition to the mounting cultural factors contributing to this world-ending event which Bruenig's reporting exposed, Hochschild points to powerful economic stressors.

> For many congregants, well-paid, union-protected jobs through which a man could support a stay-at-home wife are gone for all but a small elite. . . . For the whole bottom 90 percent of workers, average wages have flattened since 1980. Many older white men are in despair . . . . Although life expectancy for nearly every other group is rising, between 1990 and 2008 the life-expectancy of older white men without high school diplomas has been shortened by three years—and truly, it seems, by despair. In their tough secular lives, life may well feel like "end times."[15]

Within this conviction of certain near-term apocalyptic disaster, it is easy for evangelicals to choose to live for the moment. When Hochschild asked a woman evangelical leader what she thought the role of the

---

12. Bruenig, "In God's Country," 32. For a more trenchant criticism of Trump's practice of Christianity, see the Haynes' postscript "Your Bonhoeffer Moment," in *The Battle for Bonhoeffer*, 136–48.

13. Hochschild, *Strangers in a Strange Land*, 124.

14. Hochschild, *Strangers in a Strange Land*, 125.

15. Hochschild, *Strangers in a Strange Land*, 125–26.

CONCLUSIONS

Environmental Protection Agency should be in protecting the fragile marsh ecology in southwest Louisiana from environmental damage caused by the petrochemical industry, she replied, "If I had to choose between the American Dream and a toad, hey, I'll take the American Dream." Pressed for further reflection, she said, "I want my ten great-grandchildren to have a great planet, but the earth may just not be here."[16] Belief in the Rapture turns out to be the theological legitimation of the rape of the earth.[17]

Our study of 1 Peter and its being influenced by the Book of the Twelve has made us alert to expressions of people struggling to be faithful under insurmountable odds. In chapter 5 we reflected on experiences of Christians across the world. We can now add to this group the expressions of Christians chronicled by Bruenig and Hochschild. We can identify the specter of irreversible decline as a current formulation of implacable destiny. Moreover, our exegetical work sensitizes us to listen for notes of genuine abandonment voiced by evangelicals, as well as cynicism and despair, with its concomitant results of anxiety and faithlessness. While the international voices, and to a lesser degree the American ones, drew strength from the hope of the resurrection in their struggle to combat the structures opposing them, evangelicals have reduced the power of the resurrection to its barest minimum of holding on. They simply wish for government to build a wall around them within which they can get on with "their way of life."

However, this is only half of the picture. Bruenig also interviews two members of a progressive, faith-based community action group called Faith in Texas. It strives to work across denominational lines to further peace and justice issues at the local, neighborhood level. When Bruenig asked how difficult it had been to work with evangelical groups since Trump's ascendancy, she was struck by how often the responses of community organizers were laced with diabolical language to describe the push-back they encountered. One said, evangelicals are "'trying to play devil's advocate on things like the immigration policy, or 'locking up kids.' Justifying Trump's policies regardless of whether they fit into a Christian ethical framework is . . . 'very much a

---

16. Hochschild, *Strangers in a Strange Land*, 123, 125.

17. Congruent with this perspective is the recent appointment by President Trump of Paula White as his advisor to his Faith and Opportunity Initiative. This is his plan to give religious groups more of a voice in government programs devoted to issues like defending religious liberty and fighting poverty. Paula White is a noted exponent of the "prosperity gospel," a highly unorthodox ideology that God wants followers to find wealth and health. See Peters, "Newest White House Aide."

devil's bargain of like—yes, he's awful; yes, he does not represent our values; but he's allowing us to pack the courts with justices who do."[18]

This resorting to hyperbolic language referencing the devil caused Bruenig to wonder if progressives as well shared the view with Jeffress "that American Christians are destined for ever-greater cataclysms in public life, until the eventual apocalypse resolves in the return of Christ." She found that progressives did in fact "feel that they were undertaking a difficult and oftentimes, uphill battle against forces material and intangible."[19] David Brooks from his national reporting confirms this finding. "Many young voters in their OK Boomer T-shirts feel exactly the same [as do evangelical voters], except about climate change, employment prospects, and debt. This sense of elite negligence in the face of national decline is the core issue right now."[20]

One member of Gen Z voiced his frustration this way, "Essentials are more expensive than ever before, we pay 50 percent of our income to rent, no one has health insurance. Previous generations have left Generation Z with the short end of the stick."[21] Anti-boomer sentiment is fueled by rising inequality, unaffordable college tuition, and political polarization, all exacerbated by the internet and the climate crisis.

A parallel reduction in good health outcomes happens as well in these younger people who see their futures in decline. Blue Cross Blue Shield, an American health insurance company, released a report on November 6, 2019, by Moody's Analytics "The Economic Consequences of Millennial Health," which found:

> Millennials are seeing their health decline faster than the previous generation as they age. This extends to both physical health conditions, such as hypertension and high cholesterol, and behavioral health conditions, such as major depression and hyperactivity. Without intervention, millennials could feasibly see mortality rates climb up by more than 40% compared to Gen-Xers at the same age. . . . What's more, according to the CDC, accidental deaths, which include overdoses, and suicides were the cause of 60% of the deaths among 25–29 years old in 2017. A generation

---

18. Bruenig, "In God's Country," 38.
19. Bruenig, "In God's Country," 38–39.
20. Brooks, "Impeach Trump," 4. For additional commentary on the OK Boomer movement, see Bate, "Why Are Gen Z+ Millennials Calling Out Boomers on TikTok?"
21. Brooks, "Impeach Trump," 4.

before, in 2002, those two causes accounted for less than half of all deaths in the same age cohort.²²

Self-harm is a likely outcome of concluding you are living in an end-game situation.

Because this movement among young voters is so new, our evidence is largely anecdotal. Nevertheless, we venture two observations. First is that both the Ok-boomers and fundamentalist evangelicals share a mind-set that convinces them their futures in decline. It is sadly ironic that each side perceives the other as the culprits. Each side advocates for political solutions that are antithetical to the other. This will only lead to more stagnation.

The second observation is that this conviction of decline is a source of shared pain. A faith-based community organizer put his finger on the insight that much of the agony many evangelicals experience as citizens has roots in private pain: "If we're talking about Trump voters, people don't react with this kind of hatred or fear unless there's pain at the root somewhere, and if you don't address that pain, you're never going to break through the hatred and fear."²³ Remember Hochschild's observation that evangelical worship "offered a collective, supportive arena . . . within which it was safe to feel helpless, sad, or lost." The pain also comes through from the young: "Everybody in Gen Z is affected by the choices of the boomers, that they made and are still making. Those choices are hurting us and our future. Everyone in my generation can relate to that experience and we're really frustrated by it."²⁴ This pain is supported by the empirical data of increased mortality rates.

This should be impetus for those who have care of congregations to reach again for 1 Peter and its demonstration of the power of worship to address pain. Within the sphere of shared pain with Jesus, powerfully new impulses for hope can emerge. However, Hochschild's description of evangelical worship as a "collective, supportive arena . . . within which it was safe to feel helpless, sad, or lost"²⁵ does not address the pain in ways that result in energy which powers action that is innovative and redemptive.

In the national discussion that must be the foundation for any resolution, 1 Peter brings a unique perspective. Christians come to the table of the national discussion peculiarly sensitive to outcries of pain and

22. "The Economic Consequences," 3, 5.
23. Bruenig, "In God's Country," 39.
24. Lorenz, "'OK Boomer,'" 3.
25. Hochschild, *Strangers in a Strange Land*, 124.

abandonment. This sensitivity is built-in to our being embraced by a suffering Jesus. There is no room for the negligence of the elite. Astonishingly, Christians shoulder pain while being armed with an overflowing joy and confidence regarding our future. Our future is founded on the resurrection of Jesus from the ultimate decline, death. Not just any death, but a death shot through with pain and abandonment. Moreover, we see ourselves commanded to bring this future into partial but authentic expression in the present because our being embraced by the resurrected Jesus renews us to have the energy to think new thoughts, propose bold solutions, and reach across chasms. His overcoming of the ultimate decline is our inheritance, our spiritual capital which we are free to spend in this life through our work to serve others.[26]

We serve our present crisis by creating worship that encourages voiced pain and lament as we bind ourselves to the crucified Christ, and at the same time worship which is filled with eschatological joy from the resurrected Christ which bursts the cocoon of being frozen in our hurt. Our worship will not be content to distract attention from a grim present by painting a fantasy of a hoped-for future, but rather our worship will open the congregation to the possibilities of that future which is resident even now in the assembled Body of the crucified-resurrected Jesus

We serve our present crisis by committing ourselves not to be defined by our pain and hurt. Instead, we will define ourselves by how God has been faithful to us in a sheer act of grace. Is our destiny to live our "fiery trials" through the struggle against a rising tide of national depression and retreat? If so, we live knowing that instead of cynicism we can show hope, that instead of the individual scramble for survival we can show the care of a community, that instead of playing the blame game we can offer bold solutions. In a word, we can employ the eschatological qualifier to our present situation.

The question for the church is not Who is an alien? The question is Who has the strength to flourish as an alien? Who can distinguish themselves by serving humanity even as an alien? The eschatological qualifier placed on the Christian's identity by baptism into Christ and nourished through worship, prayer and study, opens access to indescribable joy whose behavioral markers are stamina, persistence, and empowerment.[27] Against

26. As an example of new initiatives emerging within white evangelical circles, see Worthen, "What Would Jesus Do About Inequality?"

27. I would also include the resources of uplifting music, by luminous art, by thoughtful cinema, by theatre that celebrates the complexity of the human condition.

the drift toward decay, the church can join with all who care for the renewing of the social contract on which this country was founded. The residents of southwestern Louisiana and all others who feel left behind in a globalized economy will find a way to thrive in the modern economy with a new sense that they are respected contributors. Moreover, OK-boomers and all others who want their democratic freedoms protected, the earth cherished, and the right to live in ethnically diverse pluralistic neighborhoods will be satisfied.[28] The church knows that we act on the basis that our future cannot decay, cannot be polluted, and cannot bleed out. 1 Peter is meant in our time for persons and communities who struggle to find the insight to respond to overwhelming odds with energy and new alternatives. "Cast all your anxiety on him, because he cares for you" (5:7).

---

28. See Brooks, "The Revolt Against Populism," 5B.

Bibliography

Abertz, Rainer. "Exile as Purification: Reconstructing the Book of the Four (Hosea, Amos, Micah, Zephaniah)." In *Society of Biblical Literature 2002 Seminar Papers*, 213–33. Atlanta: Society of Biblical Literature, 2002.

Ackroyd, Peter R. *Exile and Restoration, A Study of Hebrew Thought of the Sixth Century B.C.* The Old Testament Library. Philadelphia: Westminster, 1968.

Bailey, Warner M. *Living in the Language of God: Wise Speaking in the Book of the Twelve.* Eugene, OR: Pickwick, 2017.

———. *The Self-Shaming God Who Reconciles: A Pastoral Response to Abandonment within the Christian Canon.* Eugene, OR: Pickwick, 2013.

Balch, David L. *Let Wives Be Submissive: The Domestic Code in 1 Peter.* SBLDS, 26. Chico: Scholars, 1981.

Barnett, Victoria J. "Bonhoeffer is Widely Beloved. But to Fully Understand Him We Should First Dial Back the Hero Worship." *The Washington Post*, April 9, 2015. https://www.washingtonpost.com/news/accts-of-faith/wp/2015/04/09/bonhoeffer-is-widely-beloved-but-to-fully-understand-him-we-should-first-dial-back-the-hero-worship/

Bauckham, Richard. "James, 1 and 2 Peter, Jude." In *It Is Written: Scripture Citing Scripture: Essays in Honor of Barnabas Lindars*, edited by D. A. Carson and H. G. M. Williamson, 303–17. Cambridge: Cambridge University Press, 1988.

Bauman-Martin, Betsy. "Speaking Jewish: Postcolonial Aliens and Strangers in First Peter." In *Reading First Peter with New Eyes, Methodological Reassessments of the Letter of First Peter*, edited by Robert L. Webb and Betsy Bauman-Martin, 144–77. London: T. & T. Clark, 2007.

Bechtler, Steven Richard. *Following in His Steps: Suffering, Community, and Christology in 1 Peter.* SBLDS 162. Atlanta: Scholars, 1998.

Beentjes, Pancratius C. "The Fluidity between the Oppressed of Israel and Israel the Oppressed: Some Additional Notes to B. Gregory's Analysis of Ben Sira 35:14–26." In *"With All Your Soul Fear the Lord" (Sir 7:27)*, 65–64. Leuven: Peeters, 2017.

Ben-Porat, Ziva. "The Poetics of Literary Allusions." *PTL A Journal for Descriptive Poetics and Theory* (1976) 105–28.

BIBLIOGRAPHY

Ben Zvi, Ehud. "Twelve Prophetic Books or 'The Twelve': A Few Preliminary Considerations." In *Forming Prophetic Literature: Essays on Isaiah and the Twelve in Honor of John D. W. Watts*, edited by James W. Watts and Paul R. House, 125–56. Journal for the Study of the Old Testament Supplements 235. Sheffield, UK: Sheffield University Press, 1996.

Best, Ernest. "1 Peter 2:4–10: A Reconsideration." *Novum testamentum* 11(1969) 270–93.

Best, Payne. *The Venio Incident*. London: Hutchison, 1950.

Bethge, Eberhard. *Bonhoeffer: Exile and Martyr*. Edited by John W. de Gruchy. London: Collins, 1975.

———. *Dietrich Bonhoeffer: A Biography*. Revised and edited by Victoria J. Barnett. Minneapolis: Fortress, 2000.

Black, Max. *Models and Metaphors: Studies in Language and Philosophy*. Ithaca, NY: Cornell University Press, 1962.

Bonhoeffer, Dietrich. *"After Ten Years": Dietrich Bonhoeffer and Our Times*. Introduction by Victoria J. Barnett. Minneapolis: Fortress, 2017.

———. *Berlin, 1932–1933*. Vol. 12. Minneapolis: Fortress, 2009.

———. *The Collected Sermons of Dietrich Bonhoeffer*. Vol. 2. Edited by Victoria J. Barnett. Minneapolis: Fortress, 2017.

———. *Conspiracy and Imprisonment, 1940–1945*. Vol. 16. Minneapolis: Fortress, 2006.

———. *Discipleship, 1937*. Vol. 4. Minneapolis: Fortress, 2001.

———. *Ecumenical, Academic, and Pastoral Work, 1931–1932*. Vol. 11. Minneapolis: Fortress, 2012.

———. *Letters and Papers from Prison*. Vol. 8. Minneapolis: Fortress, 2010.

———. *Theological Education at Finkenwalde, 1935–1937*. Vol. 14. Minneapolis: Fortress, 2013

———. *Theological Education Underground, 1937–1940*. Vol. 15. Minneapolis: Fortress, 2012.

Borgen, Peder. "The Early Church and the Hellenistic Synagogue." In *Philo, John and Paul: New Perspectives on Judaism and Early Christianity*, 207–32. BJS 131. Atlanta: Scholars, 1987.

Boring, M. Eugene. *1 Peter*. Abingdon New Testament Commentaries. Nashville: Abingdon, 1999.

Brett, M. G. "Interpreting Ethnicity: Method, Hermeneutics, Ethics." In *Ethnicity and the Bible*, edited by M. G. Brett, 3–22. Biblical Interpretation. Leiden: Brill, 1996.

Brooks, David. "Impeach Trump. And Then Move On." *The New York Times*, November 1, 2019. https://www/sltrib.com/opinion/commentary/2019/11/01/david-brooks-impeach/

———. "A New Center Being Born." *New York Times*, December 20, 2018. https://www.nytimes.com/2018/12/20/opinion/centrism-moderate-capitalism-welfare.html

———. "The Revolt Against Populism." *The New York Times*, November 21, 2019. www.nytimes.com/2019/11/21/opinion/populism

———. "Will Gen-Z Save the World." *The New York Times*, July 4, 2018. https://www.nytimes.com/2018/12/20/opinion/centrism-moderate-capitalism-welfare.html

Bruenig, Elizabeth. "In God's Country. Evangelicals View Trump as Their Protector. Will They Stand by Him in 2020?" *The Washington Post*, August 14, 2019. https://www.washingtonpost.com/opinions/2019/08/14/evangelicals-view-trump-their-protector-will-they-stand-by-him/?arc404-true

BIBLIOGRAPHY

Bulkeley, Tim. "The Book of Amos as 'Prophetic Fiction': Describing the Genre of a Written Work that Reinvigorates Older Oral Speech Forms." In *The Book of the Twelve & the New Form Criticism*, edited by Mark J. Boda et al., 205-19. Ancient Near East Monographs 10. Atlanta: Society of Biblical Literature, 2015.

Carter, Warren. "'Going all the Way?': Honoring the Emperor and Sacrificing Wives and Slaves in 1 Peter 2.13—3.6." In *A Feminist Companion to the Catholic Epistles and Hebrews*, edited by Amy-Jill Levine, 14-33. London: T. & T. Clark, 2004.

Chen, Carolyn, "Accidental Pilgrims: Modernity, Migration, and Christian Conversion among Contemporary Taiwanese Americans." In *Encountering Modernity*, edited by Albert L. Park and David K. Yoo, 95-115. Los Angeles: University of Hawai'i Press, UCLA Asian American Studies Center, 2014.

Childs, Brevard S. *Isaiah*. The Old Testament Library. Louisville, KY: Westminster John Knox, 2001.

———. "Retrospective Reading of the Old Testament Prophets." *Zietschrift für die alttestamentliche Wissenschafte* 108 (1996) 162-27.

Coggins, Richard. "Interbiblical Quotations in Joel." In *After the Exile, Essays in Honor of Rex Mason*, edited by John Barton and David J. Reimer, 75-84. Mercer, GA: Mercer University Press, 1996.

Corley, Kathleen E. "1 Peter." In *Searching the Scriptures, II, A Feminist Commentary*, edited by Elisabeth Schüssler Fiorenza, 349-60. New York: Crossroad, 1994.

de Gruchy, John W. *Theology and Ministry in Context and Crisis: A South African Perspective*. Grand Rapids: Eerdmans, 1986.

Dias, Elizabeth, and Jeremy W. Peters. "Evangelical Leaders Close Ranks with Trump After Scathing Editorial." *The New York Times*, December 21, 2019. https://www.nytimes.com/2019/12/20/us/politics/christianity-today-trump-evangelicals.html

Dinkler, Michal Beth. "The Bible and Women? We Need to Talk." *Reflections*, Fall 2019, 5-7.

Dryden, J. de Waal. *Theology and Ethics in 1 Peter: Paraenetic Strategies for Christian Character Formation*. Tübingen: Mohr Siebeck, 1996.

Eco, Umberto. *The Role of the Reader: Explorations in the Semiotics of Texts*. Advances in Semiotics. Bloomington, IN: Indiana University Press, 1979.

"The Economic Consequences of Millennial Health." Blue Cross Blue Shield, November 6, 2019.

Elliott, John H. *The Elect and the Holy: An Exegetical Examination of 1 Peter 2:4–10 and the Phrase "Basileon ierateuma."* Leiden: Brill, 1966.

Feldmeier, Reinhard. *The First Letter of Peter: A Commentary on the Greek Text*. Translated by Peter H. Davids. Waco, TX: Baylor, 2008.

———. "The 'Nation' of Strangers: Social Contempt and Its Theological Interpretation." In *Ethnicity and the Bible in Ancient Judaism and Early Christianity*, edited by Mark G. Brett, 241–70. New York: Brill, 1996.

Fiorenza, Elisabeth Schüssler. *1 Peter, Reading against the Grain*. London: Bloomsbury, 2017.

Foster, Paul. "Echoes without Resonance: Critiquing Certain Aspects of Recent Scholarly Trends in the Study of the Jewish Scriptures in the New Testament." *Journal for the Study of the New Testament* 38 (2015) 96–111.

Galli, Mark. "Trump Should Be Removed from Office." *Christianity Today*, December 19, 2019/. https://www.christianitytoday.com/ct/2019/19/2019/december-web-only/trump-should-be-removed-from-office.html

BIBLIOGRAPHY

George, Larry. "1 Peter." In *True to Our Native Land: An African American New Testament Commentary*, edited by Brian K. Blount et al., 476–87. Minneapolis: Fortress, 2007.

Gertner, Meir. "Midrashim in the New Testament." *Journal of Semitic Studies* 7 (1962) 267–92.

Godsey, John D. *The Theology of Dietrich Bonhoeffer*. Philadelphia: Westminster, 1960.

Gorsline, Robin Hawley. "1 and 2 Peter." In *The Queer Bible Commentary*, edited by Deryn Guest et al., 724–36. London: SCM, 1988.

Green, Clifford. "Hijacking Bonhoeffer." *Christian Century*, October 19, 2010, 34–38.

Green, Joel B. "Faithful Witness in the Diaspora: The Holy Spirit and the Exiled People of God according to 1 Peter." In *The Holy Spirit and Christian Origins: Essays in Honor of James D. G. Dunn*, edited by Graham N. Stanton et al., 282–95. Grand Rapids: Eerdmans, 2002.

———. "Living as Exiles: The Church in the Diaspora in 1 Peter." In *Holiness and Ecclesiology in the New Testament*, edited by Kent E. Brower and Andy Johnson, 311–24. Grand Rapids: Eerdmans, 2007.

Gregory, Bradley C. "The Relationship between the Poor in Judea and Israel under Foreign Rule: Sirach 35:14–26 among Second Temple Prayers and Hymns." *Journal for the Study of Judaism* 42 (2011) 311–27.

Griffin, Horace L. *Their Own Receive Them Not: African American Lesbians and Gays in Black Churches*. Cleveland, OH: Pilgrim, 2006

Grossman, Maxine I., *Reading for History in the Damascus Document: A Methodological Study*. STDJ 45. Leiden: Brill, 2002.

Hall, Jonathan. *Ethnic Identity in Greek Antiquity*. Cambridge: Cambridge University Press, 1997.

Hauerwas, Stanley, and William H. Willimon. *Resident Aliens, Life in the Christian Colony*. Nashville: Abingdon, 1989.

Hayes, Stephen R. *The Battle for Bonhoeffer: Debating Discipleship in the Age of Trump*. Grand Rapids: Eerdmans, 2018.

Hedrick, C. W. "Jonah the Prophet (Jonah)" In *The Crosby-Schøyen Codex: Ms 193 in the Schøyen Collection*, edited by E. James Goehring, 217–59. Louvain: Peeters, 1990.

Hochschild, Arlie Russell. *Strangers in Their Own Land: Anger and Mourning on the American Right*. New York: New Press, 2016.

Holloway, Paul A. *Coping with Prejudice: 1 Peter in Social-Psychological Perspective*. Wissenschaftliche Untersuchungen zum Neuen Testament 244. Tübingen: Mohr Siebeck, 2009.

Horrell, David G. "Aliens and Strangers? The Socioeconomic Location of the Addresses of 1 Peter." In *Engaging Economics: New Testament Scenarios and Early Christian Reception*, edited by Bruce W. Longenecker and Kelly D. Liebengood, 177–202. Grand Rapids: Eerdmans, 2009.

———. "Between Conformity and Resistance: Beyond the Balch-Elliott Debate towards a Postcolonial Reading of First Peter." In *Reading First Peter with New Eyes: Methodological Reassessments of the Letter of First Peter*, edited by Robert L. Webb and Betsy Bauman-Martin, 112–42. London: T. & T. Clark, 2007.

———. "Ethnicisation, Marriage and Early Christian Identity: Critical Reflections on 1 Corinthians 7, 1 Peter 3 and Modern New Testament Scholarship." *New Testament Studies* 62 (2016) 439–60.

———. "Jesus Remembered in 1 Peter? Early Jesus Traditions, Isaiah 53 and 1 Peter 1.21–25." In *James, 1 & 2 Peter, and Early Jesus Traditions*, edited by Alicia J. Batten and John S. Kloppenborg, 123–50. London: T. & T. Clark 2014.

———. "The Label Χριστιανός: 1 Peter 4:16 and the Formation of Christian Identity." *Journal of Biblical Literature* 126 (2007) 361–81.

———. "'Race,' 'Nation,' 'People': Ethnoracial Identity Construction in 1 Pet 2.9." *New Testament Studies* 58 (2012), 123–43.

———. "The Themes of 1 Peter: Insights from the Earliest Manuscripts (the Crosby-Schøyen Codex ms 193 and the Bodmer Miscellaneous Codex Containing P72)." *New Testament Studies* 55 (2009) 502–22.

———. "Whose Faithfulness Is It in 1 Peter 1:5?" *Journal of Theological Studies* ns 48 (1997) 110–15.

Horrell, David G., et al. "Visuality, Vivid Description, and the Message of 1 Peter: The Significance of the Roaring Lion (1 Peter 5:8)." *Journal of Biblical Literature* 132 (2013) 697–716.

Jackson, Peter, and Jan Penrose. "Introduction: Placing 'Race' and 'Nation.'" In *Constructions of Place, Race and Nation*, edited by Peter Jackson and Jan Penrose, 1–12. Minneapolis: University of Minnesota Press, 1993–94.

Jeremias, Jörg. "The Function of the Book of Joel for Reading the Twelve." In *Perspectives on the Formation of the Book of the Twelve*, edited by Rainer Albertz et al., 77–88. Beihefte zur Zeitschrift für die alttestmentliche Wissenschaft 433. Berlin: de Gruyter, 2012.

Kehinde, Simeon F. "Christianity amidst Violence: An Exegesis of 1 Peter 2:4–10." *Ogbomoso Journal of Theology* 19 (2014) 78–92.

Koet, Bart J. "Elijah as Reconciler of Father and Son: From 1 Kings 16:34 and Malachi 3:22–24 to Ben Sira 48:1–11 and Luke 1:13–17." In *Rewriting Biblical History: Essays on Chronicles and Ben Sira in Honor of Pancratius C. Beentjes*, edited by Jeremy Corley and Harm van Grol, 173–190. Deuterocanonical and Cognate Literature Studies, Vol. 7. Berlin: De Gruyter, 2011.

Leuchter, Mark. "Another Look at the Hosea/Malachi Framework in the Twelve." *Vetus Testamentum* 64 (2014) 249–65.

Liebengood, Kelly. "Confronting Roman Imperial Claims: Following the Footsteps (and the Narrative) of 1 Peter's Eschatological Davidic Shepherd." In *An Introduction to Empire in the New Testament*, edited by Adam Winn, 255–72. Atlanta: Society of Biblical Literature, 2016.

———. *The Eschatology of 1 Peter, Considering the Influence of Zechariah 9–14*. New York: Cambridge University Press, 2014.

Lincoln, Ulrich. "The Perception of Dietrich Bonhoeffer in Germany." https://www.projectbonhoeffer.org.uk/the-perception-of-dietrich-bonhoeffer-in-germany/

Lorenz, Taylor. "'OK Boomer' Marks the End of Friendly Generational Relations." *The New York Times*, October 29, 2019. https://www.nytimes.com/2019/10/29/style/ok-boomer.html

Marsh, Charles. "Eric Metaxas's Bonhoeffer Delusions." *Religion & Politics*, October 18, 2016, 1–6.

———. *Strange Glory: A Life of Dietrich Bonhoeffer*. New York: Knopf, 2014.

Martin, Dale B. *Slavery as Salvation: The Metaphor of Slavery in Pauline Christianity*. New Haven, CT: Yale University Press, 1990.

McEvenue, Sean. "The Truth Trap in Interpretation." In *Seeing Signals, Reading Signs: The Art of Exegesis: Studies in Honor of Anthony F. Campbell, S.J. for His Seventieth Birthday*, edited by Mark A. O'Brien and Howard N. Wallace, 171–84. London: T. & T. Clark, 2004.

Michaels, J. Ramsay. *1 Peter*. Word Biblical Commentary 49. Grand Rapids: Zondervan, 1988.

Miscotte, Kornelis H. *When the Gods Are Silent*. Translated by John W. Doberstein. New York: Harper and Row, 1967.

Moberly, R. W. I. "God Is Not a Human That He Should Repent." In *God in the Fray: A Tribute to Walter Brueggemann*, edited by Tod Linafelt and Timothy K. Beal, 112–23. Minneapolis: Fortress, 1998.

Moy, Russell, C. "Resident Aliens of the Diaspora: 1 Peter and Chinese Protestants in San Francisco." In *Asian American Christianity Reader*, edited by Vij Nakka-Cammauf and Timothy Tseng, 267–78. Castro Valley, CA: The Institute for the Study of Asian American Christianity, 2009.

Nelson, F. Burton. "The Life of Dietrich Bonhoeffer." In *The Cambridge Companion of Dietrich Bonhoeffer*, edited by John W. de Gruchy, 22–49. Cambridge: Cambridge University Press, 1999.

Nogalski, James D. "How Does Malachi's 'Book of Remembrance' Function for the Cultic Elite?" In *Priests & Cults in the Book of the Twelve*, edited by Lena Sofia Tiemeyer, 191–212. Ancient Near Eastern Monographs 14. Atlanta: Society of Biblical Literature, 2016.

———. "Reading the Book of the Twelve Theologically: The Twelve as Corpus: Interpreting Unity and Discord." *Interpretation* 61 (2017) 115–22.

Nogalski, James D., and Ehud Ben Zvi. *Two Sides of a Coin: Juxtaposing Views on Interpreting the Book of the Twelve/the Twelve Prophetic Books*. Piscataway, NJ: Gorgias, 2009.

Pajunen, Mika S., and Hanne von Weissenberg. "The Book of Malachi, Manuscript 4Q76 (4QXIIa), and the Formation of the 'Book of the Twelve." *Journal of Biblical Literature* 134 (2015) 731–51.

Peters, Jeremy W., and Elizabeth Dias. "Newest White House Aide Is Uniquely Trumpian Pastor." *The New York Times*, November 2, 2019. https://www.nytimes.com/2019/11/02/us/politics/paula-white-trump.html

Pitts, Leonard, Jr. "Fascism: It CAN Happen Here." *Fort Worth Star-Telegram*, October 14, 2019.

Robinson, Marilynne. *The Givenness of Things: Essays*. New York: Farrar, Straus and Giroux, 2015.

Rivera-Rodriguez, Luis R. "Towards a Diaspora Hermeneutics." In *Character Ethics and the Old Testament: Moral Dimensions of Scripture*, edited by M. Daniel Carroll R. and Jacqueline E. Lapsey, 169–89. Louisville, KY: Westminster John Knox, 2007.

Schlingensiepen, Ferdinand. *Dietrich Bonhoeffer 1905–1945: Martyr, Thinker, Man of Resistance*. Translated by Isabel Best. London: T. & T. Clark, 2010.

Schutter, William L. *Hermeneutic and Composition in 1 Peter*. Wissenschaftliche Untersuchungn zum Neuen Testament, II/30. Tübingen: Mohr (Siebeck), 1989.

BIBLIOGRAPHY

Schwarz, Eberhard. *Identitat durch Abgrenzungsprozesse in Israel im 2 vorchristlichen Jahrhundert und ihre traditionsgecschichtlichen Voraussetzungen Zugleich ein Beitrag zur Erforschung des Jubildenbuches.* Europaische Hochschulschriften, Series 23 Theology 162; Frankfurt: Lang, 1983.

Sechrest, Love L. *A Former Jew: Paul and the Dialectics of Race.* London: T. & T. Clark, 2009.

Seitz, Christopher R. *Joel.* International Theological Commentary. London: T. & T. Clark, 2019.

———. "On Letting a Text 'Act Like a Man': The Book of the Twelve, New Horizons for Canonical Reading with Hermeneutical Reflections." *Scottish Bulletin of Evangelical Theology* 22 (2004) 151–72.

———. "What Lesson Will History Teach?" In *"Behind" the Text: History and Biblical Interpretation*, edited by Craig Bartholomew et al., 443–69. Grand Rapids: Zondervan, 2003.

———. *Zion's Final Destiny: The Development of the Book of Isaiah. A Reassessment of Isaiah 36–39.* Minneapolis: Fortress, 1991.

Seland, Torrey. "πάροικος καὶ παρεπίδημο: Proselyte Characterizations in 1 Peter?" *Bulletin for Biblical Research* 11.2 (2001) 239–68.

Selwyn, Edward Gordon. *The First Epistle of St. Peter.* 2nd ed. Grand Rapids: Baker, 1981.

Senior, Donald C. P. *1 & 2 Peter.* New Testament Message 20. Wilmington, DE: Glazier, 1980.

Smith, Daniel L. *The Religion of the Landless: The Social Context of the Babylonian Exile.* Bloomington, IN: Meyer Stone, 1989.

Steueragel, Valdir R. "An Exiled Community as a Missionary Community: A Study Based on 1 Peter 2:9, 10." *Evangelical Review of Theology* 40 (2016) 196–204.

Stovel, Beth M. "'I Will Make Her Like a Desert'. Intertextual Allusion and Feminine and Agricultural Metaphors in the Book of the Twelve." In *The Book of the Twelve & the New Form Criticism*, edited by Mark J. Boda et al., 37–61. Ancient Near East Monographs 10. Atlanta: Society of Biblical Literature, 2016.

Sweeny, Marvin A. *The Twelve Prophets.* 2 vols. Berit Olan: Studies in Hebrew Literature and Poetry. Collegeville, MN: Liturgical, 2000.

Thompson, M. *Clothed with Christ: The Example and Teaching of Jesus in Romans 12.1–15.13.* Journal for the Study of the New Testament Supplements 59. Sheffield, UK: JSOT Press, 1991.

Van der Merwe, Hendrik W., et al. *African Perspectives on South Africa.* Stanford: Hoover Institution, 1978.

Van Rensburg, Fika J. "Christians as 'Resident and Visiting Aliens': Implications of the Exhortations to the παροίκοι and παρεπίδημοι in 1 Peter for the Church in South Africa." *Neotestamentica* 32 (1998) 573–83.

Volf, Miroslav. "Soft Difference: Theological Reflections on the Relation between Church and Culture in 1 Peter." *Ex Auditu* 10 (1994) 15–30.

von Weissenberg, Hanne, et al. *Changes in Scripture: Rewriting and Interpreting Authoritative Traditions in the Second Temple Period.* Beihefte zur Zeitschrift für die altestamentliche Wissenschaft, 419. Berlin: de Gruyter, 2011.

———. "The Twelve Minor Prophets at Qumran and the Canonical Process." In *The Hebrew Bible in Light of the Dead Sea Scrolls*, edited by Nóra Dávid et al., 357–78. Götteingen: Vandenhoeck & Ruprecht, 2012.

Wall, Eric. "With Voices United: Singing (and other Music) in the Church." *Insights* 125 (2019) 3–16.

Watts, James W. "Psalmody in Prophecy: Habakkuk 3 in Context." In *Forming Prophetic Literature: Essays on Isaiah and the Twelve in Honor of John D. W. Watts,* edited by James W. Watts and Paul R. House, 209–23. Journal for the Study of the Old Testament Supplements 23. Sheffield, UK: Sheffield Academic Press, 1996.

Willis, William. "Letter of Peter (1 Peter)." In *The Crosby-Schøyen Codex: Ms 193 in the Schøyen Collection,* edited by E. James Goehring, 137. Louvain: Peeters, 1990.

Worthen, Molly. "Can Black Evangelicals Save the Whole Movement?" *The New York Times,* April 20, 2019, https://www.nytimes.com/2019/04/20/opinion/sunday/black-evangelicals-diversity.html

———. "What Would Jesus Do about Inequality?" *The New York Times,* December 13, 2019, https://www.nytimes.com/2019/12/13/opinion/sunday/christianity-inequality.html.

www.ingramcontent.com/pod-product-compliance
Lightning Source LLC
Chambersburg PA
CBHW051942160426
43198CB00013B/2261